It is indeed my pleasure to dedicate this work to the Almighty God from whom all wisdom and knowledge comes as a gift. People and nations perish for lack of knowledge (Hosea 4:6). I have learnt from many years of experience in life that wisdom comes from above and that the fear of God is indeed the beginning of all wisdom. What then can I say than to give God all the glory for the guidance, the vision, provisions and the courage to put this book together for current and future leaders in all sectors of the African economies.

The major aim of this book is to bring corrupt and poor leadership in Africa to an end through promotion of integrity as the key attribute for leaders and to change the attitudes of corrupt and poor leaders. It is expected that this will promote outstanding leadership in Africa generally and Nigeria in particular. This book is therefore dedicated to all those in position of leadership now and in the future. The book is also dedicated to all scholars researching on leadership and the young that shall grow to rescue Africa and Nigeria through effective leadership.

To whom much is given much is expected. African and Nigerian leaders have a lot to do to deliver the continent from underdevelopment and abject poverty. The book tries to remind them that they must earn the trust of their subordinates to remain trustworthy and effectively lead the battle in the boardroom, war front, and/or spiritual arena. The key word is integrity in leadership.

CONTENTS

FOREWORD

The Rt. Rev. Dr. James Olusola Odedeji,
Lord Bishop, Diocese of Lagos West

Upon browsing through this scholarly book by our own Dr. Isaac Ngwube on leadership integrity, my mind went straight to an anecdote on African leadership which tells of how some African leaders went to God to complain about their countries being short-changed in His distribution of natural resources which they perceived to be heavily skewed in favour of Nigeria; and God advised them to hold their peace and wait to see what Nigerian leaders would do with the resources before complaining. The inference from this story tends to suggest that God Himself is concerned about the dearth of leadership in Nigeria. Nigerians certainly know that we have leadership problem bedevilling our nation, what many don't know is what the problem actually is. The missing nexus between leadership presence and good governance in both political and economic life of the nation is what Dr. Ngwube has identified in this well researched work as the dearth of integrity in leadership. Statistical revelation of honesty as the top most characteristic of admired leaders across cross-cultural platform lends credence to the author's finding and position on this matter.

Given his conviction that integrity is the pillar around which progress and advancement revolve, one can understand why we are where we are as a nation some 60 years after independence. Incidentally, Africa has deliberately but curiously earned herself the ignoble recognition as omphalos of the notorious debacle of poor and corrupt leadership.

Dr. Ngwube has proven through this work that appears to be his magnum opus, at least for now, that doctoral degree is indeed a certification of research capacity and competence; or how else would one explain the volume and depth of research effort that went into this piece of work that is difficult to place within a particular literary genre because of its richness in historical, biblical and statistical facts blended with expert knowledge of political economy and management science. Of course, nothing short of such high standard of delivery is expected of an accomplished Management expert like Dr. Isaac Ngwube who once managed Nigeria's sphere of Management training and development.

Dr. Ngwube's submission that integrity can be learned, coupled with examples of notable Nigerians whose integrity won them international recognition and awards, seems to me a ray of hope penetrating through the dark tunnel of poor and corrupt leadership to give us hope of a better tomorrow for Nigeria and Africa at large. This, I think, aligns with the author's aim of using the instrumentality of this powerful book to "change the attitudes of corrupt and poor leaders and promote outstanding leadership in Africa generally and Nigeria in particular."

We are particularly delighted for the honor of writing the foreword to this great intellectual and impactful book of international standard by Dr. Isaac Ngwube, a highly esteemed, resourceful and trustworthy member of our Diocese. We felicitate with him on this great achievement mainly because it takes a man of integrity to dare put pen to paper on the subject of integrity, particularly when it touches on political and administrative leadership of a complex nation as Nigeria.

It is therefore to the glory of God and hope of leadership revival in Africa and Nigeria in particular, that we commend this mind illuminating book to all potential beneficiaries of the deep insights shared inter alia.
God bless you.

+Olusola Lagos West (Anglican)
Pentecost, 2020

ACKNOWLEDGEMENT

The account of this book will be incomplete without mentioning the Nigerian Institute of Management (NIM). I must acknowledge the role NIM played in making the emergence of this book possible. The Institute as an employer on my return to Nigeria from Britain in 1983, offered me a platform to get involved in thinking and planning for the training and development of Nigerian managers and leaders for better performance in both public and private sectors of Nigerian economy. I became compassionate in the pursuit of the Institute's goals and objectives. Writing and presentation of papers and discussions with participants during the courses and seminars opened my eyes to the myriads of problems of mismanagement and poor leadership in our organisations. I gradually developed a great passion for finding lasting solutions to these problems.

I spent 26 years of my active life trying to deal with these problems through training and development within the Institute until I retired as Registrar/Chief Executive of NIM, in 2009. The passion I acquired while working for the Institute refused to depart from me even after I left on retirement. I therefore decided to put this book together for posterity and legacy, and I strongly feel that the Institute and the principal officers, notably all the presidents, must be acknowledged greatly.

Having acknowledged the Institute, I must also acknowledge

the key personalities that linked me to the Institute because I believe that my arrival at the Institute was divine. I did not plan it. I want to posthumously acknowledge the first character, a gentleman of blessed memory, Mr Austin Onwudimegwu, who worked for Lintas as a graphic artist. He introudcted me to another gentleman, Mr Godstime Osaze, who was the Head of General Management Department of the Institute. Godstime became my boss in the general management department until I was transferred to the East to be the Resident Consultant in charge of the operation in Eastern Nigeria in 1988. I will not forget to acknowledge the late Martin Oworen, a brilliant scholar from Colonel University, who was the Acting Director-General of the Institute in 1983 when I was employed. He found me good enough for permanent employment.

Let me also acknowledge the role played by the University of Manchester, UK. This great citadel of learning exposed me to research skills and knowledge that led me to search for the unknown and be determined to contribute to knowledge. I appreciate the support and guidance of the professors, lecturers and supervisors in the Institute for Development Policy and Management, (IDPM) of the University of Manchester, UK, from 2003.

I must also posthumously acknowledge the role played by Late Professor Dora Akunyili. Despite her busy schedule as Director-General of NAFDAC she approved my study of NAFDAC as a case study for effective leadership in the Public sector. May her soul continue to rest in peace. I was able to interview her on the 30th of November, 2004, to gain lots of insights on why NAFDAC succeeded under her leadership. She accomplished a lot at NAFDAC and saved the lives of many Nigerians by finding and destroying many fake and expired food and drugs at the risk of her own life. May I also acknowledge Mazi Sam Ohuabunwa, the former Chief Executive of Neimeth who also allowed me to use NEIMETH as a case study for the private sector. He was another leader that I found effective on the strength of integrity in leadership within the private sector of the economy.

Finally, I will not forget to acknowledge my core family, starting from my wife, Mrs I.S. Ngwube, and, my children. They encouraged me and reminded me about this book constantly to a point of discomfort because they did not want me to give up on this book.. May God reward their efforts and make them to read and learn so much from this book and join the great leaders of tomorrow.

CHAPTER ONE

Introduction

Many writers and researchers alike have continued to express different views on leadership for over a century now. Leadership studies have been going on for a long time and we can see this as a very old field of studies that kept demanding for more, due to dynamism in our world and the insatiable and changing nature of man. The problem of leadership is widespread in our world today but more pronounced in Africa where greed and corruption has become the order of the day. In the past, the position of leadership had been the preserve of men and women of integrity who proved to be servant leaders with passion for the good of the society and comfort of all mankind. This is no longer the case in Africa, as failures of leadership can easily be noticed and felt in both private and public sectors of the economy. The value system has gone down the drain and get- rich- quick syndromes have taken over. African leaders, especially the political leaders have mastered rhetoric, and this has become their stock in trade. Their political statements and manifestoes are quite often a package of lies and deceits that are devoid of truth and yet they will always claim to be men and women of integrity.

The western world remained better off because they took time to develop and promote effective leadership in their systems. They established and promoted democratic leadership and it worked well for them because they built strong institutions that ensures that the rules remain intact. African societies failed mainly because there were no strong institutions to preserve the rules. The emergence of military governments in Africa made the matter worse by destroying the few existing institutions deliberately to perpetrate selfish intensions. The military leadership gave birth to political leaders that lack integrity completely and have great appetites for amassing wealth and impoverishing the societies. Otherwise how else can one explain the massive failures in Nigeria, of infrastructure, insecurity of lives and properties, increase in poverty and unemployment all over the country on one hand and the sudden emergence of extremely rich politicians on the other hand. The wealth suddenly appeared without established industries or verifiable source of legitimate income.

Most of these political leaders were not able to pay the salaries of government workers under them and yet they were able to amass wealth for themselves in such a primitive manner. These are not leaders but economic saboteurs that should be rejected and sent packing. Africa and Nigeria in particular, needs leaders that have integrity in the real sense of it, if they want to come out of the mess of underdevelopment and poverty in the midst of plenty natural resources. It is very common in Nigeria to see ex-governors, ministers and commissioners becoming guests of the EFCC after leaving office. The common way out is for most of them to find their way to the National Assembly in continuation after leaving office to ensure continuous immunity or influence. All these are disheartening and strong evidence that many leaders in Africa lack integrity and therefore have failed their societies. There is an urgent need to go back to the drawing board to get the leadership requirements right. Integrity, an innate quality has been found through research work to be the pillar that holds and promotes outstanding leaders.

The Build Up of the Challenges

My life experience and exposures, especially during my university days in Britain and long career in management training and development at the Nigerian Institute of Management (NIM) for twenty six years were the combined forces that arrested my thoughts and compelled one to think of how to get involved in the promotion of better leadership in Nigeria. It has therefore been a long-lasting worry and question of why Nigeria should remain underdeveloped despite the abundance of natural resources.

The worries and passion for change grew as I progressed in my career. The more I interacted with managers and leaders during training sessions the more worried I became, because I was seeing deep-rooted problems that kept defying solutions. The participants were aware that the problems of corruption and poor leadership exist everywhere. They knew that the situation was bad but felt helpless and defeated. It was like, "let the sleeping dog lie".

The more I moved on and up in my career, the more disturbed I felt. I decided that I would address the problem personally one day. I moved up to head various directorates like, Directorate of Training, Research and Consultancy Services, Directorate of Corporate Services, and Human Resources. The challenge for changes became more pronounced. At this stage, I found opportunity to put integrity into practice in my leadership roles at the various directorates I headed. The experience was found to be fulfilling and first hand confirmation that leadership with integrity promotes trust amongst the led and the leader. It promotes outstanding results within the organisation.

Finally when I became the Chief Executive of NIM, I was exposed fully to the challenges of poor leadership in the country. I decided that I would do something to fight this failed leadership in the country and that I would not be part of those that would rather allow the sleeping dog to lie. Practically as the Chief Executive, I pursued the Institute's goal fully and continued in my leadership efforts to promote integrity and made it the watch word in all ramifications within the Institute.

However, modesty and decorum demand that one should not blow his trumpet. The official records of achievements should rather be allowed to speak. As the head of the Corporate Services Directorate in 2005, I was given the enormous tasks of implementing the NIM/NYSC strategic partnership initiated by the late President of NIM, Chief LEA Aimiuwu, who was a brilliant strategist. May his soul rest in peace. The Institute had to establish and run learning centres for youth corpers in all the 36 states of Nigeria at the same time. This project was to exist for over a year before any meaningful breakeven. Integrity in action and effective team leadership gave NIM the breakeven and wonderful results within six months.

It is therefore in fulfilment of the promise to fight failed leadership that this book was put together. It is a gift to the young and future generation of potential leaders that should strike the final blow to failed leadership in Nigeria and Africa. To ensure a resounding and reliable success, I was forced to rise up to this great challenge by way of further research in leadership. The developed countries of the world were found to be showing good examples of effective leadership in both private and public sectors of their economies.

Their leaders were found to be disciplined and able to abide by the rules of engagement. The developed countries were able to establish strong institutions to control and regulate activities of leaders and followers. The leaders in the developed countries of the world were not allowed to break the rules and get away with it easily. They were not allowed to destabilise the strong institutions put in place. The regulatory and controlling roles of these institutions were allowed to remain effective and leaders operating in such environment are forced to comply with the rules of the game and maintain integrity expected of leaders. Such leaders remained disciplined to deliver effective results most of the time. In these societies any false or corrupt behaviours were easily discovered and the culprits punished appropriately.

This is not so in African countries where most of the institutions established for control and regulatory purposes are deliberately made to fail by the political leaders. African political leaders are known to have a penchant to work on weakening established institutions meant for controlling them. This can easily explain why the executive arm of the government would always want to reduce the powers and independence of the judiciary and the legislature. The agencies of government are often deliberately made to function like toothless bull dogs. The weakness of the judiciary and legislature enables the executive to get stronger to the point of dictatorship. This ensures that when the executive falls short of expectation it could still carry on as if nothing went wrong and nobody could have the guts to challenge it. The failed African political leaders would never resign or apologise for any failure because of lack of integrity and accountability. They would rather use all the powers at their disposal to fight to stay put in office rather than resigning.

However, there is no doubt that Africa and Nigeria in particular have gifted potential leaders in abundance. They are intelligent, with vision and courage. All they need is empowerment and a full dose of integrity. They need to be encouraged that acts of integrity would always be rewarded adequately. When the men and women of integrity arrive at the positions of leadership, Africa and Nigeria will be transformed within a short period. I have done serious research into the root cause of the failures of leadership in Nigeria in order to make meaningful contributions on the way forward. I discovered that the trait theory in leadership is still relevant to the Nigerian need for improvement in leadership capability. Africa and Nigeria need men and women with integrity to take over the leadership positions and deliver the long-expected results that will transform the continent. Appointing or accepting leaders without established integrity to remain in office will keep Africa and Nigeria in perpetual slavery of underdevelopment and poverty.

The Theoretical Framework Of The Research

The trait theory having been found appropriate for the research has been chosen. At this point we therefore have need to revisit the trait theory of leadership which has a lot to do with the innate qualities of a leader, to see what could be learnt to tackle the problem of failed leadership in Nigeria and Africa in general. The author has therefore reviewed the works of some of the early writers and researchers on trait theory of leadership such as Stogdil (1948, 1974), Mana (1959), Burns (1978), Adair (1983), Lord Devader and Alliger (1986), Kotter (1988), Kirkpatrick and Locke (1991) and Covey (1992).

The Great Man Theory

The "Great Man Theory" propounded by Galton (1869 and cited in Albert, 2003), is a good confirmation that leadership study had been on for a long time. This theory assumes that there are some leadership traits innate to man, and to this end, it is argued that leaders are born but not made. This argument had however, been countered by Kirkpatrick and Locke (1991) who argued that individuals could be born with these traits, they could learn them, or both. We must agree that these views are quite helpful and fundamental in the study and development of leadership because it can be debated strongly as presented in the literature reviews in chapter two of this book. The literature reviews were part of the author's earlier research on leadership for a PhD programme, successfully completed and defended at the University of Manchester, United Kingdom, in 2007.

It must be clearly stated here that I am strongly convinced that leaders can be born and can also be made through relevant development programmes. I believe that leaders can improve their ability and quality through continuous learning and development. I am of the opinion that leaders that lack integrity could improve through change of attitudes or repentance and determination to offer better and honest services that will leave good legacy for posterity. It is possible to be brought up by disciplined and upright parents who could impart good character and integrity. Positive environmental factor could be of tremendous help too. The environment could also influence one negatively. A man or woman of integrity may come under heavy corrupt pressure and may fall for corruption. It is also possible that a person with low or no integrity can come under positive pressure that can transform the person to emerge with high level of integrity. Experience in manpower development and general management training shows that employees can be developed and transformed at different levels. Therefore, there is hope that a bad society can be changed if corrective measures are put in place.

Nevertheless, the focus of this book is not on whether leaders are born or made. Bryman (1992) defines leadership in terms of social influence where the leader steers members of a group towards a goal. By this definition leadership involves influence and this could be positive or negative. This influence in Nigeria has been more of negative than positive and this is the fundamental problem of leadership in Nigeria and Africa.

We need to concentrate on the missing link that have caused massive failures in all sectors of leadership in Nigeria, and in Africa generally. We have witnessed serious and consistent failures in political leadership with the dire consequences. It is the same story in public and private sector organisations. The leadership in the police and the military are not spared from this general malaise.

What can we say about the judiciary, the legislatures and even the regulators like the Economic and Financial Crimes Commission (EFCC) and Independent Corrupt Practices Commission (ICPC)? All the sectors have failed due mainly to lack of integrity and transparency. Unfortunately, the leadership of the religious bodies that should show light have also joined the bandwagon. Nigerian banks have also been failing and collapsing for many years due mainly to mismanagement and leadership with little or no integrity. The failures of these banks were taking place despite the banks' reputation for recruiting high flyers for the top job and the very tight control measures usually in place.

All these failures call for urgent and serious review of the situation and immediate re-orientation that will ensure that those that will aspire for any position of leadership in Nigerian organisations and even for political leadership must be proved to be men and women of integrity before they are appointed or voted in. This problem should be tackled strategically from the entry points by subjecting prospective leaders to integrity test which is now available as reported in chapters five and six.

Looking at this problem from the theoretical framework of trait, it must be agreed that effective leaders must basically have courage, knowledge of the job, intelligence, self-confidence, determination and vision, but integrity should henceforth be a must for all. It will henceforth not be enough for prospective leaders to pretend to have integrity by mere usage of the word. They must be able to walk the talk because the test of the pudding is in the eating. The massive failures in leadership in Nigeria and Africa in general have made integrity the most important trait that the leaders must have in addition to the basic requirements.

Integrity is considered key to success in leadership, but it has not been given enough or specific attention, may be, because it is considered abstract. This notwithstanding, we have been able, through research efforts, to find ways round about it, to argue that integrity is the issue in leadership in Nigeria and Africa and can be researched on effectively, as we have done. The Cambridge English dictionary defines integrity as the quality of being honest and having strong moral principles that you refuse to change.

Having integrity means doing the right thing in a reliable way. It is personality trait that we admire, since it means a person has a moral compass that does not waver. It is about being honest and having strong moral principles. Integrity is a weapon for effective leadership that leaders often neglect and treat as old fashioned. However, the truth must be told, that both political as well as leaders in private organisations have failed to deliver good results especially in this 21st century because they lost the trust of their followers or subordinates.

Let us face the facts, the subordinates or followers of the 21st century are smarter and better informed now and access to information technology is a boost to their enlightenment. The followers now have the ability to know when the leader embarks on lies and deception. The hidden agenda of the leader can easily be exposed technologically. The situation is calling for immediate change and leaders of today must realise that it is no longer business as usual and should therefore change for good.

Integrity in leadership has been pushed to the back burner in our modern society and the consequences are enormous and glaring for all to see especially in Nigeria. Efforts must therefore be made to recover the lost inestimable jewellery of effective leadership in a corrupt environment where failures of leaders have brought untold hardship and virtual collapse of the system. David, an old outstanding and well documented leader, as was recorded in the Bible (Psalm: 25, verse 21) so many thousands of years ago said "May integrity and upright-ness protect me, because my hope is in you".

The society has lost moral values and positive direction, be-cause the leaders have opted for propaganda and promotion of falsehood rather than upholding the truth which remains the hallmark of integrity and effective leadership. They have failed to lead by positive example and there are mistrust, agi-tations and insecurity everywhere. The leaders have lost the trust of their followers because they failed to be trustworthy. This book is therefore an effort towards the recovery. It is focusing and highlighting the importance and effect of integ-rity in result-oriented leadership. It is presenting this reliable trait as the required weapon for conquering subordinates or followers' mistrust. We have noticed that intimidation can-not deliver effective results on continuous and consistent basis. The leaders' intimidation is a weak weapon that can only last for short period under the cover of eye-service and sycophancy with no results. Propaganda and rhetoric have not helped leaders and managers these days, because 21st century fol-lowers are better informed. This is a modern trend and cannot be reversed and the earlier we come to terms with this, the bet-ter progress we can make in every front as leaders. It is better to hold unto the truth because it will remain consistent unlike falsehood. Above all the truth has a way of setting us free all the time. The 21st century leaders and managers must rise to this challenge and make the difference. This book is not a means of destroying existing leaders but an instrument for correction and redirection.

We have witnessed civilisation and changes in our world, but nothing has changed the truth. Over two thousand years ago it was recorded in the bible that the truth and nothing but the truth shall set us free (John 8:32). We must learn from history and be wiser for it. The failures in the world today in the areas of leadership and management can easily be traced to failure to accept the truth. Truthfulness has a strong link with integrity and it can therefore be said that where there is no truth there is no integrity.

This for sure should be an eye opener to those leaders who claim to have integrity and make noise about it without actions to back it up. Modern leaders often embark on fruitless journey of cover up and false impression by hiring communication experts and media advisers for packaging and presenting falsehood to deceive the public. They forget that we are living in a modern world that is called global village, where information technology has made communication easier than ever before. Facts are readily available and window dressing is no longer acceptable. It is more glaring by the day that for modern leaders to succeed, they must be transparently honest to win the trust of their followers. They need facts more than fable.

This trait known as integrity is quite rare and difficult to possess. Nevertheless, it takes discipline, determination, training and courage to develop and possess it. When possessed, it must be protected because it has many enemies that will be willing to destroy it at the slightest opportunity. Integrity is light-bearing and throws light into the world of darkness and corruption. The people of the world today has moved much closer towards darkness and corruption and there is so much ill-gotten wealth and resources to show for it and this makes it irresistible and attractive to many. Invariably, there is trouble and failures everywhere. Promotion of integrity in leadership is the way out.

Respected authors have made lots of contributions on effective leadership and have said much. Notably, Kouzes and Posner (2002), said that leadership depends on trust. It has also been said that trust is the product of trustworthiness (Adair, 1983). Kouzes et al went further to state that if people anywhere are to willingly follow someone – whether it be into battle or into the boardroom, the front office or the front lines – they first want to assure themselves that the person is worthy of their trust.

People want to know that the person is truthful, ethical, and principled. According to them, no matter what the setting, everyone wants to be fully confident in their leaders, and to be fully confident they must believe that their leaders are people of strong character and solid integrity. Apart from these, it may interest readers to note that integrity is not a new topic as such but very old and have been of help to outstanding leaders of old.

Think about the success of some of the outstanding leaders recorded in the bible, like Joseph, Moses, Joshua, David, Daniel and Paul. Joseph is an interesting case study for discussion here because of the process he went through. A brief review of Joseph's performance will show that he did not waver in maintaining integrity and the fear of God in all his leadership roles throughout his life, even in a foreign land, Egypt, where he was sold into slavery due to his senior brothers' act of jealousy and wickedness. The details about Joseph's life and leadership abilities in a strange land could be found in the bible, precisely from Genesis (chapters 37, and 39 to 50). It is not necessary to dwell too much on Joseph here because we only need to highlight his performance in leadership with strict application of integrity and fear of God.

When he arrived in Egypt, he was only seventeen years old and was bought as a slave by Potiphar, one of the Pharaoh's officials, the captain of the guard. His master found him reliable and subsequently made him a leader in charge of his household. He led uprightly and effectively but not without challenges. The most outstanding and devastating of all was the master's wife who forcefully wanted to sleep with him. He refused and forcefully ran out of the house because he believed in integrity and feared God and wanted to remain consistent in character and faithful to his master. This refusal landed him in serious trouble because the seductive wife of his master got offended and disappointed. Her next action was blackmail as a cover up. She raised false alarm and accused Joseph of attempted rape and her husband believed her and put Joseph in jail.

We should not be surprised and discouraged about this because this is the kind of challenges effective leaders with integrity should expect. When upright leaders try to maintain the standards and truthfulness there will be some oppositions and distractions. This is not failure on its own but what matters is the consistency of the leader and the ability to overcome the challenges. We are not dwelling on theory because this is common in our society today. Leaders with genuine integrity are bound to face challenges especially in a highly corrupt society.

A man or woman of integrity must be consistent in character and actions and be able to stand the test and overcome the challenges. The ability to overcome the challenges remains a source of strength and authority for the leader subsequently. From experience, we can testify on the magnitude of respect and admiration that follow men and women of integrity even after retirement. Leaders with integrity may be blackmailed and suffer some setbacks like Joseph did in Egypt, but their future achievement will remain remarkable and outstanding. They will always come out stronger and even their detractors will admire their courage and achievement privately if not openly.

Joseph moved on later and increased in wisdom and ability to deliver good results and subsequently became the prime minister of Egypt. As prime minister, he delivered wonderful results that favoured Egypt as a country and by extension his country of origin and the brothers that sold him to slavery in the first place. We cannot beat the reach of leadership with integrity. The other historical leaders like Moses, Joshua, David, Daniel and Paul have a lot in common with Joseph. They followed the footsteps of Joseph and the fear of God and the clamour for truth and uprightness remained their guiding principles. They all recorded outstanding performances and good successes. The modern leaders should not see these as irrelevant historical accounts of success in leadership because truthfulness will always prevail because it holds the keys and power to success in everything we do in this world.

Anybody in doubt should check out the late Nigerian Professor Dora Akunyili's leadership success in the National Agency for Food and Drug Administration and Control, NAFDAC, from 2001 to 2004 when she was the Director-General of the organisation. Within this short period, she accomplished what all her predecessors in that office could not achieve from the inception of NAFDAC. She applied integrity in her leadership and won the trust and confidence of her subordinates. I can say this categorically because I conducted a research on her leadership role at NAFDAC and had the privilege of interviewing her and good number of the Directors who were her immediate subordinates during her tenure.

I cannot say much about her political role as minister of information, after she left NAFDAC because I did not research on that. One thing that was clear to me and many Nigerians at that time, was that she was effective and delivered wonderful results where many have failed. She succeeded there because she consistently maintained uprightness and led by example. After her exit from NAFDAC, a successor came in but could not sustain the tempo since the weapon of integrity could not be continuously applied, and the organisation got back to square one. We can say it loud and clear that there is no short-cut to success in leadership other than leadership with integrity even in our modern world. It is not a matter of choice because corrupt, wicked and godless leaders will always fail. It is just a matter of time.

Modern Day Failures In Leadership

Unfortunately, modern day leaders have not learnt from history. General Sani Abacha was once a very powerful and intimidating military/ political leader in Nigeria. He was a military head of state that took over after General Babangida. He sacked Shonekan's few months interim government and was feared by many because he was ruthless and behaved like a god. But the man died. His death was unexpected. He did not die in battlefield like a soldier but within the comfort zone of the presidential seat of Aso Rock, Abuja, as was reported by government press. The lesson here is that we have no better choice in leadership than to fear God because he holds our breath in his palm and can close the palm anytime.

Those who maintained continuous success like Joseph as stated above, were reported to be consistent and continuous with the truth and fear of God in their approach to leadership. This in a way is pointing to the fact that the practice of integrity must be consistent and continuous for success to be maintained. It is a continuum. There is a big lesson for all leaders of today to learn from those who have failed in the past, irrespective of whether they are political, organisational and or religious leaders. There are statistical evidence and research results on leadership and integrity as presented by the author in chapters five and six of this book.

Poor Development/Slow Growth
– Dishonesty In Leadership

The countries of the world are witnessing and suffering for lack of integrity in leadership and management. There is no doubt that this problem is more pronounced in Nigeria and other African countries. This can explain the terrible slow pace of development and stunted growth in Africa irrespective of huge natural resources deposited within the continent. The only visible evidence that Africa and Nigeria have huge deposits of mineral resources, can be traced to the number of billionaires without portfolios of productive ventures, parading about and intimidating the society.

This failure is widespread and no sector or level is spared as stated earlier. Whether it is under the political parties PDP or APC in Nigeria, it is the same story. There may be multiplicity of churches and mosques in Nigerian cities but these have failed to promote and produce men and women of integrity that can lead with the fear of God in our society. It can be more devastating to note that the citadels of knowledge have also failed the test of good leadership. The vice chancellors, rectors, and other leaders of our higher institutions have not lived up to expectation, hence the continuous downfall of the standard and quality of education all over the place.

Education is key to development and nurturing of future leaders, and if we get this wrong, every other thing can easily go wrong. The motivation to write this book is borne out of passionate desire to contribute and kickstart the revolution in leadership in our country and in our continent. I therefore strongly hope that this effort will not be in vain.

CHAPTER TWO

*LITERATURE REVIEW
ON LEADERSHIP*

It could be said that lots had been done by leadership experts and so a lot could be learnt from the previous works of experts in leadership studies. This chapter is therefore devoted to the presentation and discussion of the literature relating to leadership with particular focus on the trait approach to leadership in the light of leadership at organizational level. The contributions of experts on trait theory and other leadership theories and approaches like the works of Stogdill, Mann, Burns, Lord Devader, and Alliger, Northouse, Bryman, Kirkpatrick and Locke, Adair, Kotter, Kouzes and Posner, Covey, Goleman, and others, will be presented and discussed. These will be analysed and comparison made to show the relevance of trait approach, and integrity to leadership. As stated by Barrientos (1988), the reviews will help to relate to the new aspects of inquiry or in other words will throw more lights to the new area of interest.

Kotter (1988) stated that leadership has always been and probably always will be an important factor in human affairs, but despite this, there has been some misunderstanding of what it is all about. According to him leadership is used in two basic ways in everyday conversation. The first refers to the process of moving a group of people in some direction through mostly non-coercive means, and the second refers to people who are in roles where leadership (the first definition) is expected. As stated in chapter one, Bryman (1992) defined leadership in terms of process of social influence whereby a leader, steers members of a group towards a goal. By Bryman's definition leadership involves influence. It is concerned with how the leader affects followers, and the leader is the focal point.

Fafowora et al (1995) also see leadership as implying a purposeful direction of the affairs of the led – some movement towards definite and defined goal which will be to the benefit of the society and such leadership is characterized by imaginativeness (i.e. possessing ideas which can be translated into reality), courage (to stand on principle and by its decisions as to be able to provide moral, social and motivational climate for its followership) and discipline. Here again the qualities required refer to the leader and not the followers, and the movement towards definite and defined goal is expected to be led by the leader. Olusanya (2002) said that positive leadership involves influencing people and institutions towards well defined goals, which contributes to the betterment or greater well-being of society and is characterized by imagination, creativity, discipline, courage and integrity. It is interesting to note from this definition too that integrity is given as one of the traits the leader is expected to possess in order to influence the followers towards the expected goal. Northouse (2001) on the other hand stated that despite the multitude of ways that leadership has been conceptualized, several components can be identified as central to the phenomenon of leadership. According to him, they are: (a) leadership is a process; (b) leadership involves influence; (c) leadership occurs within a group context; and (d) leadership involves goal attainment. Based on these components, Northouse (2001) defined leadership as a process whereby individual influences a group of individuals to achieve a common goal.

From all the above it becomes quite clear that leadership involves responsibility and is not a mean task. The success or failure rest on the shoulders of the leader because from the above definitions and explanations a lot is expected from the leader who appears to be the key factor, and it is clear that the leader needs the trust of the followers (Kouzes and Posner, 2002) to succeed in organizational setting. The need for integrity could therefore not be over-emphasized. It could therefore be argued that trait approach to leadership which focuses exclusively on the leader and not the followers or the situation is justifiable for the effective study of leadership.

Allen (1998), stated that leadership studies can be classified as trait, behavioural, contingency, and transformational, and that earliest theories assumed that primary source of leadership effectiveness lay in the personal traits of the leaders themselves. The trait approach was therefore one of the first systematic attempts to study leadership (Northouse, 2001) and it focuses exclusively on the leader, and not the followers or the situation, and in the early 1900s, leadership traits were studied to determine what made certain people great leaders. The trait approach suggests that organizations will work better if the people in managerial positions have designated leadership profiles (Northouse, 2001). In line with this argument, Allen (1998) stated that trait theories intended to identify traits to assist in selecting leaders since traits are related to leaders' effectiveness in many situations. The trait approach to understanding leadership supports the use of tests and interviews in the selection of managers, and this involves attempting to match the traits and characteristics of the applicant to the positions (Allen, 1998). All these assumptions are quite supportive and make the trait approach the suitable theoretical framework for this work.

Man (1959 cited in Northouse, 2001) suggested that personality traits could be used to discriminate leaders from non-leaders, and he identified leaders as strong in traits like intelligence, masculinity, adjustment, dominance, extroversion and conservatism. Lord et al (1986) reassessed the findings of Mann (1959), but, according to Northouse (2001) using a more sophisticated procedure called meta-analysis, found that intelligence, masculinity, and dominance were significantly related to how individuals perceived leaders. Lord et al (1986) therefore argued strongly that personality traits could be used to make discriminations consistently across situations between leaders and non-leaders (Northouse, 2001). The review by Kirkpatrick and Locke (1991) also argued for the importance of leadership traits and contended that leaders are not like other people. A qualitative synthesis of earlier research by them, gave rise to six traits such as: drive, the desire to lead, honesty and integrity, self-confidence, cognitive ability, and knowledge of the business. According to Kirkpatrick and Locke (1991), these traits make leaders differ from non- leaders. They argued further that individuals can be born with these traits, can learn them or both.

The summary of all the traits identified by various researchers from the trait approach was produced by Northouse (2001) and is shown below as table 3.1., and it illustrates the breath of traits related to leadership. Some of these appear in several of the survey studies, whereas others appear in only one or two studies, however, regardless of the lack of precision in the table, it represents a general convergence of research regarding which traits are leadership traits (Northouse, 2001). According to Northouse, a century of research on the trait approach has given rise to the extended list of traits that "would-be" leaders might hope to possess or wish to cultivate if they want to be perceived by others as leaders. Northouse (2001) further produced the second table, also reproduced below as table 3.2., containing: intelligence, self-confidence, determination, integrity, and sociability as some of the traits that are central to the list. It is worthy of note that integrity made the list, and this is the vital trait that this research is focused on.

TABLE 3.1. **Studies of Leadership Traits and Characteristics**

Stogdill (1948)	Mann (1959)	Stogdill (1974)	Lord, DeVader, and Alliger (1986)	Kirkpatrick and Lock (1991)
Intelligence	**Intelligence**	**Achievement**	**Intelligence**	**Drive**
Alertness	Masculinity	Persistence	Masculinity	Motivation
Insight	Adjustment	Insight	Dominance	Integrity
Responsibility	Dominance	Initiative		Confidence
Initiative	Extroversion	Self-Confidence		Cognitive Ability
Persistence	Conservatism	Responsibility		Task Knowledge
Self-confidence		Cooperativeness		
Sociability		Tolerance		
		Influence		
		Sociability		

Source: Reproduced from Northouse, P.G. (2001).

TABLE 3.2.	Major Leadership Traits
	Intelligence
	Self-confidence
	Determination
	Integrity
	Sociability

Source: Reproduced from Northouse, P.G. (2001).

Criticisms Of Trait Approach And The Outcome

Northouse (2001) stated that the trait approach was challenged in the mid- 1900s by research that questioned the universality of leadership traits. Stogdill (1948), in a major review suggested that no consistent set of traits differentiated leaders from non -leaders across a variety of situations. By this he means that a person with leadership traits who was a leader in one situation might not be a leader in another situation. As a result of this, leadership was re-conceptualized as a relationship between people in a social situation. Personal factors were still considered important as far as leadership is concerned but as a result of this development, researchers felt that they should be considered as relative to the requirement of the situation.

Trait approach has therefore been criticized for failing to take situations into account. Stogdill (1948) pointed out that it is difficult to isolate a set of traits that are characteristic of leaders without factoring situational effects into the equation as well. According to Stogdill, people with certain traits that make them leaders in one situation may not be leaders, given another situation. Despite the criticisms personal factors related to leadership continued to be important, but Northouse (2001) stated that researchers contended that these factors were to be considered as relative to the requirements of the situation. Reportedly, research on traits spanned the entire 20th century, but a good overview of this could be found in two surveys by Stogdill (1948, 1974). In the first survey, Stogdill analyzed and synthesized more than 124 trait studies that were conducted between 1904 and 1947 (Northouse, 2001). In the second study, he also analyzed another 163 studies that were completed between 1948 and 1970 (Northouse, 2001).

According to Northouse, Stogdill's first survey identified a group of important leadership traits that were related to how individuals in various groups became leaders. His results according to Northouse, showed that the average individual in the leadership role is different from an average group member in the following ways: (a) intelligence, (b) alertness, (c) insight, (d) responsibility, (e) initiative, (f) persistence, (g) self-confidence, and (h) sociability. The findings of Stogdill (1948) also indicated that an individual does not become a leader solely because he or she possesses certain traits, but that the traits that leaders possess must be relevant to situations in which the leader is functioning.

However, Northouse (2001) reported that Stogdill's (1974) second survey report analyzed 163 new studies and compared the findings of these studies to the findings he had reported in his first survey. According to Northouse, the second survey was more balanced in its description of the role of traits and leadership. The first survey implied that leadership is determined principally by situational factors and not personality factors (Stogdill, 1948), but the second survey argued more moderately that both personality and situational factors were determinants of leadership (Stogdill. 1974). The summary of this is that the second survey validated the original trait idea that the leader's characteristics are indeed a part of leadership (Northouse, 2001). This was quite an interesting development and a sort of confirmation of the old statement that good product will always sell itself. Relevant traits such as integrity can therefore be said to be fundamentals for effective leadership in every situation.

Bryman (1992) stated that in recent years, there has been resurgence in interest in the trait approach – in explaining how traits influence leadership. According to Northouse (2001), based on a new analysis of much of the previous trait research, Lord De Vader, and Alliger (1986) found that personality traits were strongly associated with individuals' perceptions of leadership. In the same light Kirkpatrick and Locke (1991) have gone further to claim that effective leaders are actually distinct types of people in several key respects. According to Northouse (2001) further evidence of renewed interest in the trait approach can be seen in the current emphasis given by many researchers (like Bass, 1990; Bennis & Nanus, 1985; Nadler & Tushman, 1989; Zaleznik, 1977) to visionary and charismatic leadership. This has to do with transformational leadership which Allen (1998) argued is the blend of behavioral theories with a little dab of trait theories. A transformational leader instills feelings of confidence, admiration and commitment in the followers, but this is not possible without trust (Kouzes and Posner, 2002), and trust exists if the leader has integrity which in turn is a trait. The trait approach is alive and well (Northouse, 2001). According to Northouse, it began with an emphasis on identifying the qualities of great persons; next, it shifted to include the impact of situation on leadership; and most currently, it has shifted back to reemphasize the critical role of traits in effective leadership.

Research on traits was also criticized for failing to look at traits in relationship to leadership outcomes. In other words, it has emphasized the identification of traits, but failed to address how leadership traits affect group members and their work. The trait researchers have also been criticized for focusing on the link between specific traits and leader emergence but failing to link leader traits with other outcomes such as productivity or employee satisfaction. In line with this the trait research does not provide data or evidence to show if leaders with high intelligence and strong integrity would have better results than leaders without these traits. Some of these weaknesses highlighted above, provided the challenge and the opportunity for this study to contribute to knowledge in the field of leadership.

This study is focused on specific assessment of the effects of the integrity of the chief executives on the organizations and the subordinates within the Nigerian context. Integrity here is seen as an important and emerging trait that leaders in the third world country like Nigeria may possess in order to possibly overcome the problem of mistrust that seems to prevent effective leadership in these countries. Adair (1983) had earlier been quoted in chapter one and in more details below as reporting that many writers on leadership have stressed the importance of integrity which Viscount Slim defined as "the quality which makes people trust you". Other writers on leadership like Covey (1992) and many other recent research surveys reported below were all pointing to the importance of integrity as a trait that leaders need to gain the trust of their followers.

The above criticisms of trait approach, however, was what led to focusing of research efforts in some new directions and the subsequent emergence of the style approach to leadership (Fleishman, 1973), situational approach (Hersey and Blanchard, 1969a; Hersey and Blanchard, 1977, 1988; Blanchard, Zigarmi, & Nelson, 1993) and the contingency approach (Fiedler, 1964, 1967; Fiedler & Garcia, 1987). The style approach differs from the trait approach by emphasizing the behavior of the leader rather than the personality characteristics.

The shift in emphasis, according to Fleishman (1973), was from thinking about leadership in terms of traits that someone has, to the conceptualization of leadership as a form of activity. According to him the style approach focuses exclusively on what leaders do and how they act. By the shift to leadership style or behaviors, study of leadership in this case has therefore been expanded to include the actions of leaders toward subordinates in various contexts. The summary of the findings of researchers studying this approach showed that leadership is made up of two types of behaviors known as task and relationship behaviors.

Accordingly, task behavior helps the accomplishment of goal by group members while the relationship behavior, help them to feel comfortable with one another, themselves and within the situation they are in. Some of the studies conducted on style approach were mainly the Ohio State University in the late 1940s. This was however, based on Stogdill's earlier work which criticized trait approach and pointed to the importance of considering more than leaders' traits in research concerning leadership.

The other notable and important studies on this are the University of Michigan Studies and Blake and Mouton of 1964, 1978, and 1985. These explored how managers used these behaviors within the organizations and how leadership functioned in small groups. By looking at the findings of studies on style approach it became convincing that this had contributed further to the understanding of leadership and that there was need to consider more than leaders' traits in research concerning leadership.

However, these findings had not actually done anything to destroy the fact that the leadership traits are the fundamentals that leaders should possess before they could understand situations and apply their cognitive ability to adopt and apply appropriate style in a given situation. Apart from this, style approach had also received its dose of criticisms. For example Yukl (1994) criticized that the results from the massive research effort have been mostly contradictory and inconclusive. He pointed out that the only strong finding about leadership styles was the fact that followers of considerate leaders were more satisfied. Amongst other criticisms the approach was also criticized because it could not find a universal style of leadership that could work for all situations. It also implies that the most effective style is the high-high style, which means high task and high relationship. It is however, not practicable to apply this in all situations.

The situational approach on the other hand was developed by Hersey and Blanchard (1969a) based on the management style theory of Reddin (1967). This had been refined and revised many times since it was conceptualized (Hersey and Blanchard, 1977, 1988). This approach focuses on leadership in situations and was based on the fact that situations differ and therefore demand different kinds of leadership. For effective leadership in this approach, it is expected of the leader to adapt his or her style according to the demand of the situation.

This stresses that leadership is made up of directive and a supportive dimension and these have to be applied in the right proportion in any given situation for leadership to be effective. This requires that the leader should evaluate every situation to determine the level of competence and commitment of the subordinates for the given tasks. As a result of the varying levels of the skills and motivation of subordinates the situational leadership approach expect leaders to vary and match their styles with the competence and the level of commitment of their followers in any given situation. In this case the effective leaders are those who can recognize the needs of the employees and adopt the appropriate style to meet such needs.

According to Fiedler and Chemers (1974), contingency theory is a leader-match theory. Contingency was developed by Fiedler by studying the styles of many different leaders who worked in different context. It tries to match leaders to appropriate situations. The understanding of the performance of a leader in this approach depends on the understanding of the situations in which the leader functions. Effective leadership here is therefore contingent on matching a leader's style with the right context. Leadership styles are classified as task-motivated and relationship-motivated in the contingency theory.

The task-motivated leaders are said to be more concerned with the achievement of goals while the relationship-motivated ones are more concerned with developing interpersonal relations. For the measurement of the leadership styles Fieldler developed the LPC (Least Preferred Co-Worker) scale, and those who score high on this scale are regarded as relationship motivated while those with low score are seen as task motivated (Northouse, 2001).

The theory also suggests that three factors like leader-member relations; task structure; and position power identify three situations (Northouse, 2001). The leader-member relations refer to the loyalty, atmosphere of the group, the degree of confidence, and the attraction that exists between the leader and the followers. When the subordinates trust, like and get along very well with their leader and the atmosphere is positive, the leader-member relations are defined as good, while if opposite is the case, the relations are defined as poor (Northouse, 2001). The other variable known as task structure is to do with the degree to which the requirement of task is clear. For example, a simple and well defined task is seen as completely structured. It tends to give opportunity for more control of such task to the leader.

On the other hand a task that is not straight and clear makes absolute control by the leader in that situation difficult and is referred to as an unstructured task. The position power is the third characteristic of situation and refers to the amount of power the leader has to punish or reward subordinates. The position power is high if the leader can hire and fire or promote without any problem (Northouse, 2001).

It is however, weak if there is no such power in a given situation. These three situational factors determine whether the situation is favourable or not in organizations. The situation rated most favourable are those having good leader-follower relations, defined tasks, and strong leader position power, while the one rated least favourable are the one with poor leader-follower relations, unstructured tasks, and weak leader position power. The moderate one will be expected to fall between the two situations (Northouse, 2001). The contingency theory therefore posits that in certain situations certain styles can be effective.

In practice, the prediction on whether the leader is going to be effective in a given situation can be made using the LPC score of the leader and the three situational variables. The contingency has been criticized for what Fielder (1993) called "black box" problem as a result of level of mystery that remains concerning why task-motivated leaders are good in extreme cases while the relationship-motivated leaders perform well in settings that are moderate. Amongst other criticisms it has also been criticized for being cumbersome to use in real-world settings.

Having gone through all these various concepts and theories of leadership as explained above, it could be said that they are quite interesting and could be useful in interpreting and studying leadership to some extent. However, their limitations and nature make it difficult for any of them to fit appropriately into the focus of this research.

The trait theory remains the most appropriate for this research exercise because despite all the criticisms, in the recent years there has been resurgence of interest in the trait approach (Bryman, 1992) as a result of several reviews that have taken place. According to Northouse (2001) the trait approach is alive and well.

This research is therefore focusing on the effects of the leader's traits (especially integrity) on the subordinates and the organization's performance and productivity, so as to prove that a particular trait can bring about a desired change in an organization in a given context.

Other Relevant Research Works:

Result-Based Leadership Approach

Ulrich, Zenger and Smallwood (1999), argued that it was not enough to gauge leaders by personal traits such as character, style, and values. They said that it was a mistake to focus on leadership attributes that managers bring to the office, such as analytic thinking, working with ambiguity, and personal integrity. They are of the opinion that effective leaders know how to connect these leadership attributes with leadership results. They advocate for results-based leadership approach which is leading for attributes and results. Ulrich et al arguments could not be said to be against the trait approach (Northouse, 2001) argument that organizations will work better if the people in managerial positions have designated leadership profiles. Their arguments were quite supportive and they have stated the obvious by highlighting the importance of results. They suggest that leaders must strive for excellence in both attributes and achieving results. They gave the Results-Based Leadership formula as:

"Effective Leadership = Attributes x Results." Each term of the equation multiplies each other and they are not cumulative. For example, a score of 9 out of 10 in attributes multiplied by 2 out of 10 in results will yield effectiveness rating of only 18 out of 100 and not 11 out of 20. This simply shows that when attribute alone is high and result is low the leadership effectiveness will be low. This indeed supports the argument of this research, because the essence of good attribute is for the achievement of outstanding results. Kirkpatrick and Locke (1991) contend that leadership traits make some people different from others. In Ulrich et al results-based leadership approach, it takes high attributes and high results for the leader to be an effective leader and be different from others. In trait approach it is already assumed that leaders in organization with designated profiles (Northouse, 2001) will be effective and will produce high results.

Emotional Intelligence

Daniel Goleman (1998), the author of Emotional Intelligence argued that IQ and technical skills are important, but emotional intelligence is the sine qua non of leadership. This is another way of looking at the leadership issue which tends to play down on the trait approach (Northouse, 2001). Goleman said that effective leaders are alike in one crucial way – they all have a high degree of emotional intelligence. He gave the illustration of the highly skilled executive who was promoted into a leadership position only to fail at the job and the case of someone with solid but not extraordinary intellectual abilities and technical skills who was promoted into a similar position and then soared. Goleman did not give full details of the attributes of the effective leader without extraordinary intellectual abilities or the nature of the organization. He did not confirm that the ineffective leader possessed what Northouse (2001) call the major leadership traits The illustrations, according to him, support the widespread belief that identifying individuals with the "right stuff" to be leaders is more art than science. To him, the personal styles of superb leaders vary. Some leaders are subdued and analytical others shout their manifestos from the mountaintops. He argued that different situations call for different types of leadership, and this is very much the line of argument of Stogdill (1948, 1974). Goleman (1998) supported his points by giving example that most mergers need a sensitive negotiator at the helm, whereas organizations facing turnarounds problem require a more forceful authority. It can be argued that effective leaders basically are expected to be flexible enough to manage situations appropriately and so Goleman's points have not removed the importance and the effects of personal factors. The argument that organization will work better if the people in managerial positions have designated leadership profiles (Northouse, 2001) still stands convincingly.

Goleman argued further that IQ and technical skills are relevant but that they are mainly as "threshold capabilities", in other words, that they are the entry level requirements for executive positions. He said that his research along with other recent studies clearly shows that emotional intelligence is the sine qua non of leadership, and that without it, a person can have the best training in the world, an incisive, analytical mind, and an endless supply of smart ideas, but he still won't make a great leader. According to him, in the course of the past year, they have focused on how emotional intelligence operates at work and have examined the relationship between emotional intelligence and effective performance, especially in leaders. Goleman has analyzed competency models from 188 companies with the objective to determine which personal capabilities drove outstanding performance within the organizations, and to what degree they did so. According to him he grouped capabilities into three categories like pure technical skills like accounting and business planning, cognitive abilities like analytical reasoning, and competencies demonstrating emotional intelligence such as the ability to work with others and effectiveness in leading change.

According to him the competency models were created by psychologists who asked senior managers at the companies to identify the capabilities that typified the organization's most outstanding leaders. They also created other models by using objective criteria such as division's profitability to differentiate the star performers at senior levels within their organizations from the average ones. The stars were then extensively interviewed and tested to compare their capabilities, and this process resulted in the creation of lists of ingredients for highly effective leaders which ranged from seven to fifteen items, and included such items as initiative and strategic vision. It is important to point out here that initiative is one of the traits mentioned by Stogdill (1974), and strategic vision has a lot in common with self-confidence and determination (Northouse, 2001). According to Goleman when he analyzed the data he found that intellect was a driver of outstanding performance, and that cognitive skills such as big-picture thinking and long-term vision were particularly important, but that when he calculated the ratio of technical skills, IQ, and emotional intelligence as ingredients of excellent performance he found emotional intelligence to be twice as important as the others for jobs at all levels. It is again important to note that intellect has been classified as a trait (Stogdill, 1948; Mann, 1959; Lord, DeVader, and Alliger, 1986; Northouse, 2001). The basis for the calculations of the ratio was not clearly stated by Goleman and bias may therefore not be ruled out entirely. Goleman has also claimed that emotional intelligence is the sine qua non for effective leadership. He also claimed that other researchers have confirmed that emotional intelligence not only distinguishes outstanding leaders but can also be linked to strong performance. He gave the late David McClelland (1996) findings, as an example. He grouped capabilities into three categories like purely technical skills like accounting and business planning, cognitive abilities like analytical reasoning, and competencies demonstrating emotional intelligence such as the ability to work with others and effectiveness in leading change. It could be observed that ability to work with others and effectiveness in leading change could be argued to be the same as sociability, self-confidence and determination mentioned as major leadership traits (Stogdill, 1974; Kirkpatrick & Locke, 1991; Northouse, 2001). These should be seen as a fundamental requirement of any leader which is already assumed in the trait approach. It does not seem to be new but a matter of usage and arrangement of words. For example self-confidence is a trait, so are integrity and strong drive to achieve (Stogdill, 1974; Kirkpatrick & Locke, 1991).

Leadership Styles Theory - Goleman

Goleman, Boyatzis and Mckee (2002), expressed the view that good leaders are effective because they create resonance. Resonance comes from the Latin word resonare, to resound. They said that effective leaders are attuned to other people's feelings and move them in a positive emotional direction. They speak authentically about their own values, direction and priorities and resonate with the emotions of surrounding people. According to Goleman et al, under the guidance of an effective leader, people feel a mutual comfort level. It has been argued earlier that a leader with integrity would make the followers to develop the trust and be ready to follow anywhere (Adair, 1983; Kouzes and Posner, 2002).

According to Goleman et al (2002) resonance comes naturally to people with a high degree of emotional intelligence (self-awareness, self-management, social awareness and relationship management) but involves also intellectual aspects. This point of view is quite in agreement with Goleman (1998). They argued further that creation of resonance can be done in six ways, leading to Six Leadership Styles, and typically, the most effective leaders can act according to and skillfully switch between the various styles depending on the situation. This argument sounds interesting but it is important to draw attention to an earlier argument and conclusion by Yukl (1994) concerning multitude of studies conducted by researchers from both Ohio State University and the University of Michigan trying to find how best leaders could combine their task and relationship behaviours to maximize the impact of these behaviours on the satisfaction and performance of followers. The researchers were in essence looking for a universal theory of leadership that would explain leadership effectiveness in every situation (Northouse, 2001). Yukl (1994) stated that the results that emerged from this large body of literature were contradictory and unclear. Despite the fact that research in this area was inconclusive, Misumi (1985) stated that some of the findings pointed to the value of a leader being both high-task and high-relationship oriented in all situations.

Nevertheless, the six styles according to them are: Visionary; Coaching: Affiliative: Democratic: Pacesetting; and Commanding. By their explanation visionary leader inspires, believes in own vision, empathetic, explains how and why people's efforts contribute to the 'dream'. This style is appropriate when changes require a new vision, or when a clear direction is needed for radical change. In coaching style, the leader listens, helps people to identify their own strengths and weaknesses, counsels, encourages and delegates. This style is appropriate for helping competent, motivated employees improve performance by building long-term capabilities. The affiliative promotes harmony, nice, empathetic, boosts moral and solves conflicts. It is appropriate in situation that requires healing rifts in a team, motivate during stressful times, or strengthen connections. The democratic style involves superb listening, team working. The leader here is a collaborator, and influencer. The style is appropriate for building buy-in or consensus, or to get valuable input from employees. The pacesetting involves strong drive to achieve, high own standards, initiative, but is low on empathy and collaboration. It is impatient, micro-managing, and number-driven. It is appropriate for getting high-quality results from a motivated and competent team. The commanding style is: "do it because I say so". It is threatening, tight control, monitoring studiously, creates dissonance, contaminates everyone's mood, and drives away talent. It is only appropriate in a crisis, to kick start an urgent turnaround, or with problem employees. It is appropriate for traditional military situation.

The above accounts have emphasized the importance of situational consideration in leadership. The valid argument is that leaders should possess the appropriate traits, and this is fundamental in effective leadership. Effective leader should be able to lead well in different situations by applying the appropriate style the situation demands (Stogdill, 1974) to ensure effective leadership. It could therefore be said that this paper is more or less a shift in emphasis from thinking about leadership in terms of traits that someone has to the conceptualization of leadership as a form of activity (Fleishman, 1973).

Seven Surprises For New Chief Executive Officers (Ceos)

The Seven Surprises for New Chief Executive Officers (CEOs) is a contribution on leadership by Professor Porter, Lorsch, and Nohria (2004), as a result of their research at the Harvard Business School. The title is very catchy but it has not reduced the importance or given enough challenge to the trait approach argument that organizations will work better if the people in managerial positions have designated leadership profiles (Northouse, 2001). Although they reported that even the best prepared new chief executives can be blindsided by the realities and limitations of the job. According to them some of the surprises for new CEOs arise from time and knowledge limitations – there are so much to do in complex new areas, with imperfect information and never enough time.

Others stem from unexpected and unfamiliar new roles and altered professional relationships. According to them still others crop up because of the paradox that the more power you have, the harder it is to use. They said that while several of the challenges may appear familiar, they have discovered that nothing in a leader's background, even running a large business within his company, fully prepares him to be CEO. Most of these surprises could be challenged bearing in mind that we are advancing the arguments that selecting top managers with the appropriate traits (Northouse, 2001; Kouzes & Posner, 2002; Kirkpatrick and Locke, 1991; Stogdill, 1974) will ensure the effective performance of the organizations. It could therefore be argued that the surprises would be applicable to the new chief executive officers without the appropriate traits. However, the study made a relevant discovery and has further enforced the point that leadership role is a difficult task that requires basically people with relevant traits that will help them to cope with the expected challenges. It is also important to note that the dynamism due to changing business environment should always be taken into consideration because this is capable of springing surprises.

Porter et al reported that through their work with new chief executives of major companies, they have found seven surprises to be the most common and that how well and how quickly new CEOs understand, accept, and confront them will have a lot to do with the executives eventual success or failure. As stated above, the seven surprises highlight realities about the nature of leadership that are important not just for CEOs but for executives at any level and in any size organization.

Nevertheless, Porter et al stated that the surprise number one is that the CEO cannot run the company. They said that despite the fact that the new chief executive officers are skilled at running businesses and had looked forward to running the entire organization, they discover quickly that running the business is but a small part of the job. In running workshop for the new CEOs at Harvard Business School the participants were asked to describe what the job feels like to them. From the responses, it became clear that a new CEO's comfort and familiarity with internal operations quickly recede as demands on the executive mount. The sheer volume and intensity of external demands take many by surprise. According to them almost every new CEO struggle to manage the time drain of attending to shareholders, analysts, board members, industry groups, politicians, and other constituencies. Those hired from outside struggle to learn how their new company operates, but those promoted from within work equally hard to separate themselves from operations and learn the terrain of their outside constituencies. They reported that some told them frankly that they felt a sense of loss because they were no longer as close to the business as they were once. This can be seen as practical realities that chief executives should face in their organizations as leaders. They need to adjust to be able to face the challenges of having to take care and influence (Bryman, 1992) all the followers in their organizations and the wider stakeholders within the limited time available. The new chief executives refer to this in the report, as managing the dual roles of "Mr Inside and Mr Outside", and they were apprehensive about it. They realized that they have to let go many responsibilities like operating the company and monitoring everyone. Bennis and Nanus (1985) maintain that there is a significant difference between managing and leading. According to them to manage means to accomplish activities and master routines, while to lead means to influence (Bryman, 1992) others and create visions for change. The CEOs referred to in this study seemed to be involving themselves too much with routine operations and probably need to develop skills and the ability to delegate effectively.

The second surprise according to the report is that irrespective of the fact that the CEO is the most powerful person in any organization, using this power to issue order unilaterally is very costly. This can trigger resentment and defensiveness in colleagues and subordinates. Porter's report stated that the CEO actually reduces his real power, saps his energy and that of the organization, and slows down progress. They advised that when CEOs wield direct power, they must do so very selectively and deliberately – and never without a broader plan of action in mind. They said that usually, power is best used indirectly, through the disciplined processes otherwise it undermines the subordinate's self-confidence as well as the authority with the subordinates and peers. These in turn would create more jobs and bottlenecks for the chief executives. Although they called this surprise number two but it should not be a surprise because all along it has been assumed that effective leadership is to do with the ability to influence (Bryman, 1992) and take members of the group along to the pre-determined goal. It involves team efforts and this requires that the chief executive must be willing to share power and trust members of the group to make important decisions on behalf of the group.

The surprise number three according to them is that it is hard to know what is really going on. By this they mean that CEOs are flooded with information, but reliable information is surprisingly scarce because all information coming to the top are filtered sometimes with good intentions, and sometimes without good intentions. Receiving solid information becomes more difficult because the relationships of the chief executive with the former peers and subordinates would normally change. This should not be surprising because the chief executive has the position power and power is the capacity or potential to influence (Northouse, 2001). It is therefore normal in organizational setting for everybody to be struggling to impress the chief executive who has the power to promote or fire. Nobody would like to bring bad news to the chief executive because each person is conscious of the chief executive's assessment. This was the reason many CEOs in the Harvard Business School workshop found that unbiased information could not come from subordinates but was available from external channels, like contact with customers, conversations with other CEOs, and affiliations with industry associations, and independent advisers who could tell the unabashed truth and can criticize the thinking of the chief executive without fear.

The surprise number four is that the chief executive is always sending a message. According to this report the typical new chief executive knows that his actions will be noticed by those in his company. However, what he does not generally realize is the extent to which his every move, both inside and outside the organization will be scrutinized and interpreted. They said that the chief executive's words and deeds, no matter how small or big, are instantly spread and amplified, and sometimes drastically misinterpreted. This should be seen again as the effect of influence (Bryman, 1992). The first big message according to them is the appointment itself. The background of the chief executive and previous experiences are tools for the development of assumptions and expectations and these are strong messages on their own. All these show that messages are already on even before the actual resumption of the chief executive. It therefore means that the new CEOs once on the job cannot afford to have speculative discussions with employees because according to Porter, any half-baked idea they put across runs the risk of being latched onto as a good one, as a result of influence, and even an innocent question may be interpreted as a loss of confidence.

The implication of all these is that the new CEOs need to learn quickly what signals they are sending. According to Porter et al this knowledge will help them minimize inadvert messages and maximize the impact of the messages they want to send, once they understand the multiplier effect of their words and actions. They also need to appreciate that their decisions and actions on issues are clear messages especially to their subordinates on what they stand for and the standard they expect from them. However, having reviewed all these it is important to add that these should not really be seen as surprise as it supports the trait theory (Northouse, 2001), especially the point that influence (Bryman, 1992) is the sine qua non of effective leadership. The chief executive actions and utterances are therefore expected to be taken serious by the subordinates who are expected to be influenced by them. It is therefore in order, to expect that chief executive with the relevant traits will be able to react appropriately to the challenges as they come.

The surprise number five explained that the chief executives are not the boss. It said that many new CEOs initially assume that they have finally reached a position where they have ultimate authority, but that they soon learn that the situation is much more complicated than that. This is because the CEO may sit at the top of the management hierarchy, he still reports to the board of directors. The argument here needs no challenge especially in a world where Good Corporate Governance is the order of the day inorder to enhance accountability and performance of those entrusted to manage corporations (The Commonwealth Association for Corporate Governance (CACG), 2000). However, it must be for the interests of the new CEOs who have no experience in organizational and board politics. It is quite clear that the board hired him or her and could also fire him or her. The board has the power to evaluate the performance, set the compensation, overturn the strategy, and make other major decisions. This is indeed a serious challenge that chief executives, both new and old must face, but again this could not be said to be new in organizational terms. The board formulates the policies for the organization and the management headed by the chief executive has the duty to implement the policies, and this has all along been the practice. The only thing that is new is that the duties of the board are getting more emphasized and the directors are held more accountable for their responsibility than ever before due to increasing demand for good corporate governance being witnessed all over the world. Leadership is part of the principles of good corporate governance (CACG, 2000) requiring that every corporation should be headed by an effective board which should exercise leadership, enterprise, integrity and judgement in directing the corporation inoder to achieve continuing prosperity and to act in the best interest of the enterprise in a manner based on transparency, accountability and responsibility (CACG, 2000).

It is interesting to note that Porter and his colleagues under this, at the end agreed that the board and not the CEO is in charge. They advised that as the chief executive develops the boardroom relationships, the directors should neither be viewed as friends nor confidants but as bosses who hold the CEO personally accountable for the success of the company. They concluded that a new CEO who is open with (and creates the opportunity to collaborate with) the directors will be more likely to garner support from these bosses. Openness here implies transparency and integrity and the argument in this study has been that leadership will be effective if people with relevant traits, especially integrity, are appointed to the top position. Part of the task of this research is to prove that the exemplary leadership and the integrity of the chief executive influences the subordinates positively and also affects the productivity and the overall performance of the organization. Effective leadership depends on trust (Kouzes and Posner, 2002) and we have argued earlier that trust is the product of the trustworthiness (Adair, 1983) of the leader. It can therefore be said that a new chief executive who is trustworthy will not find it difficult to achieve good results despite the fact that the board is in charge, provided the board is carried along through regular briefing and turning board meetings into participatory discussions by the chief executive.

The number six surprise is that pleasing shareholders is not the goal. Porter et al argued that new CEOs often mistakenly believe that their primary responsibility is to keep the shareholders happy, but according to them, the problem is that defining one's goal as shareholder approval may not be in the company's best interest. This they said is because actions and strategies favored by shareholders may not benefit the ultimate competitive position of the company because shareholders come and go and they care only about what happens to the stock during the period they expect to own it. They estimated that shares in the United States for example are held for less than a year. The shareholders are therefore prone to take a short-term view and unfortunately this does not help the longer-term performance of the company. They therefore advised that CEOs need to concern themselves with creating sustainable economic value, and recognize that ultimately, it is only long-term profitability that matters, not today's growth expectations or even the stock price. According to them a high stock price will eventually collapse without the underpinnings of fundamental competitive advantage.

All the above arguments are very much in order. These are more so when we consider the widening range of stakeholders in any given business today. It will therefore be wrong for any chief executive to focus on pleasing the shareholders only. This should indeed not be a surprise to them but should be seen as fundamental lessons new chief executives should learn in a dynamic business environment. They need to focus on more than the shareholders and have longer-term success and competitive advantage in mind.

The surprise number seven according to Porter et al (2004) is that the CEOs are still only human. They said that we often view them in the cinematic image of indefatigable superhero, and yet they remain bound by all-too-human hopes, fears, and limits. They reported that the executives in their workshop have been remarkably forthcoming about the personal impact of being a CEO. Incidentally they have been able to come to terms with the fact that they could not do everything well. Accordingly, they have found it difficult and ego-bruising to accept gaps in their expertise and admit that the job of chief executive is more physically and emotionally tasking than any other jobs they have held. This is the real confirmation that they are humans. It is however, not a surprise and should not be seen as such. Chief Executive is a normal human appointed to the position of leadership mainly because of the possession of relevant traits (Northouse, 2001). It is essential for new CEOs to make a disciplined effort to stay humble, to revisit their decisions and actions, to continue to listen to others, and to find people who will be honest (Kouzes & Posner, 2002) and forth-right. It is acceptable that they need connections to the world outside their organizations at home and in the community, to avoid being consumed by their corporate lives.

Leadership As A Relationship

Kouzes and Posner (2002) as two leadership experts argued in their leadership challenge that leadership is an identifiable set of skills and practices that are available to everybody and not just a few charismatic men and women. They challenged the "great person" – woman or man – theory of leadership as plain wrong. Put moderately they say the theory that there are only a few great men and women who can lead us to greatness is just plain wrong. They consider the women and men in their research to be great and added that those with whom they worked were equally great. They argued that it is because we have so many – not so few – leaders that we are able to get extraordinary things done on a regular basis, even in extraordinary times. According to them, their findings also challenge the myth that leadership is something that you find only at the highest levels of organizations and society. They said they found it everywhere during their research work. The interesting point about Kouzes and Posner arguments that relate very well to the arguments of this research is the support of the point that leaders are not only born but can equally be made (Kirkpatrick & Locke, 1991) through development, training and exposure at all levels. This is pointing to the direction that subordinates or workers could be trained and be made to imbibe the relevant qualities or traits (Northouse, 2001) that will make them to produce the desired results. Their argument that leaders are found everywhere may not be correct, except if argued differently that potential leaders who may be trained and developed may be found everywhere. Professor Kotter (1988), in his work on the leadership factor, argued similarly that the age-old topic of leadership has become more salient recently because of important shifts in the business environment; that leadership is no longer just the domain of the Chief Executive Officer or a few top managers, but is increasingly needed in virtually all managerial jobs. He argued further that most firms today have not come close to adapting to this new reality, and that successful adaptation requires changes in a few dozen managerial practices; and that such change does not come easily, but when it does come, it can serve as a powerful source of competitive advantage.

Kouzes and Posner (2002) found this discovery inspiring and said that this should give everyone hope. Hope, because it means that no one needs to wait around to be saved by someone riding into town on a white horse. Hope, according to them, because there is generation of leaders searching for the opportunities to make a difference. Hope, because right down the block or right down the hall there are people who will seize the opportunity to lead you to greatness. They said that these people could be neighbours, friends, or colleagues, or anybody. All these again are interesting argument in support of the fact that leaders can be born and can also be made. It is a sort of assurance that third world country like Nigeria currently experiencing poor leadership (Achebe, 1984; Olusanya, 2002) may find solution to their problems through leaders who should be trained and developed to possess the designated leadership profiles (Northouse, 2001) like integrity. In other words leaders could not only be born but could be trained and developed (Kirkpatrick and Locke, 1991) everywhere, and they could be made to see integrity as a virtue that they need to develop to enable them command the respect and gain the trust of the followers (Adair, 1983). Kouzes and Posner (2002) said that the crucial truth about leadership which is more apparent today than it was before is that leadership is a relationship. According to them they have known this for a long time but have come to prize its value even more today as a result of interviewing leaders and reading their cases and the message remaining clear throughout every situation and every action. They have evidence for this point of view, for example in examining the critical variables for success in the top three jobs in large organizations, Jodi Taylor and her colleagues at the Centre for Creative Leadership found the number one success factor to be "relationship with subordinates". They reported that in an on-line survey, respondents were asked to indicate, among other things, which would be more essential to business success in five years - social skills or skills in using the internet. According to them 72% selected social skills and 28% selected internet skills. Leadership as a relationship as expressed by Kouzes and Posner has a lot to offer in leadership study but has again not rendered the trait theory useless but can be seen to be supportive. For example social skills seen here as the more essential to business success in five years has already been included as one of the major leadership traits (Northouse, 2001; Stogdill, 1974).

Kouzes and Posner (2002) went further to say that leadership is a reciprocal process between those who aspire to lead and those who choose to follow. They investigated the expectations that constituents have of leaders and asked constituents to tell them what they look for and admire in a leader. According to their report they began their research more than two decades ago by surveying thousands of business and government executives, and asked open-ended question: "What values (personal traits or characteristics) do you look for and admire in your leader?" In response to this question, respondents, according to them identified more than 225 different values, traits, and characteristics. This study is interestingly like trait study earlier done (Mann, 1959; Stogdill, 1974; Lord, DeVader, and Alliger, 1986; Kirkpatrick and Locke, 1991; Northouse, 2001) and tends to agree with trait approach to leadership. According to them they went further to do content analysis by several independent judges, followed by further analyses to reduce these items to a list of twenty characteristics with a few synonyms for clarification. According to them, they have administered this questionnaire to over seventy-five thousand people around the globe, and do update the findings continuously. They distribute the checklist and ask respondents to select the seven qualities that they "most look for and admire in a leader, someone whose direction they would willingly follow." This again fitted well into the concept of leadership without coercion but with willingness which is part of the focus of this research.

The results of their surveys have been consistently regular and striking over the years. It shows that any person wanting to be a leader must pass several tests before others are willing to grant the title of a leader to him or her. The data on table 3.3., below are very clear for further analysis. All the characteristics on the table receive some votes meaning that each is important to some people. But from 1987 to 2002, and across the continents only four characteristics or traits have continuously received over 50 percent of the votes.

Table 3.3. Characteristics of Admired Leaders.
Percentage of Respondents Selecting that Characteris

Characteristic	2002 Edition	1995 Edition	1987 Edition
HONEST	88	88	83
FORWARD-LOOKING	71	75	62
COMPETENT	66	63	67
INSPIRING	65	68	68
Intelligent	47	40	43
Fair-minded	42	49	40
Broad-minded	40	40	37
Supportive	35	41	32
Straightforward	34	33	34
Dependable	33	32	33
Cooperative	28	28	25
Determined	24	17	17
Imaginative	23	28	34
Ambitious	21	13	21
Courageous	20	29	27
Caring	20	23	26
Mature	17	13	23
Loyal	14	11	11
Self-Controlled	8	5	13
Independent	6	5	10

Source: The Leadership Challenge by James M. Kouzes and Barry Z. Posner (2002).

Note: These percentages represent respondents from six continents: Africa, North America, South America, Asia, Europe, and Australia. The majority are from the United States.

In the 1987 edition, Honest came top with 83%, followed by Inspiring with score of 68%, followed by Competent with score of 67%, and followed by Forward-looking with the score of 62%. The 1995 edition showed Honest coming top again with an increased score of 88%, followed by Forward-looking with the score of 75%, Inspiring came third with the score of 68%, followed by Competent with the score of 63%. The 2002 edition which is the latest, again showed that Honest maintained the lead with 88%, followed by Forward-looking with 71%, followed by Competent with the score of 66%, followed by Inspiring with the score of 65%. From 1987 to 2002, all the four traits remained on top as the best four, but Honest alone remained consistently as the most important trait in this research.

This shows that for people to follow someone willingly as a leader, the majority of the followers must believe that the leader is (a) Honest; (b) Forward-looking; (c) Competent; and (d) Inspiring. All these are traits and have been mentioned earlier by researchers on trait theory (Kirkpatrick & Locke, 1991; Northouse, 2001). Table 3.4., below shows some Cross-Cultural Comparisons of the Characteristics of Admired Leaders. In Australia for example Honest was selected as the most important trait with 93%, followed by Forward-looking with 83%, Inspiring with 73% and Competent with 59%. In Canada, Honest and Forward-looking came top with both scoring 88%. In Japan Forward-looking came top with the score of 83%, and Honest came second with 67%. In Korea Forward-looking came top with the score of 82%, and Honest came second with the score of 74%. In Malaysia, Honest came top again with the score of 95%, followed by Forward-looking with the score of 78%. Honest also came top in Mexico with 85%, followed by Forward-looking with 82%. In New Zealand Honest and Forward-looking both came top with the scores of 86%. For Scandinavia, Inspiring came first with the score of 90%,followed by forward-looking with 86%, while Honest came third with the score of 84%. In Singapore, Inspiring came first with the score of 94%, while Forward-Looking and Competent both came second with 78%. For the United States, it was Honest that came top with the score of 88% while Forward-looking came second with 71%. Out of the ten countries used for the cross-cultural comparisons, Honest came first in six countries, and second in four.

Table 3.4.: Some Cross-Cultural Comparisons of the Characteristics of Admired Leaders. **Percentage of Respondents Selecting Each Characteristic**

Country	Honest	Forward-looking	Competent	Inspiring
Australia	93	83	59	73
Canada	88	88	60	73
Japan	67	83	61	51
Korea	74	82	62	55
Malaysia	95	78	62	60
Mexico	85	82	62	71
New Zealand	86	86	68	71
Scandinavia	84	86	53	90
Singapore	65	78	78	94
United States	88	71	69	63

Source: The Leadership Challenge by J.M. Kouzes and B.Z. Posner, (2002).

According to Kouzes and Posner's studies, in almost every survey they have conducted, honesty has been selected more often than any other leadership characteristic, overall it emerges as the single most important ingredient in the leader-constituent relationship. According to them the percentages vary, but the final ranking does not. Right from the beginning of their studies in the early 1980s till 2002, honest has been at the top of the list. Honest as a characteristic appear top in almost all the cultures. It can therefore be said that the concept of leadership as a relationship is very much in agreement with the trait approach to leadership. The leader is expected to be honest for the followers to be able to trust him or her (Adair, 1983). Honesty here is the same thing as integrity, and Kouzes and Posner (2002) confirmed this when they said that when people talk to them about the qualities they admire in leaders, they often use "integrity" and "character" as synonymous with honesty. All these ratings and confirmations of honesty as the most important trait from different cultural backgrounds are very good support for the argument that honesty or integrity is a very important leadership trait that will likely help the chief executive to have a positive influence on the subordinates as well as the productivity and performance of the organization under his or her control.

Kouzes et al went further to state that it is clear that if people anywhere are to willingly follow someone – whether it be into battle or into the boardroom, the front office or the front lines – they first want to assure themselves that the person is worthy of their trust. People want to know that the person is truthful, ethical, and principled. According to them, no matter what the setting, everyone wants to be fully confident in their leaders, and to be fully confident they have to believe that their leaders are people of strong character and solid integrity. That nearly 90 percent of constituents want their leaders to be honest is a message that all leaders must take to heart, according to them. They concluded that honest, forward-looking, competent, and inspiring are the characteristics that have remained constant during two decades of growth and recession, the surge in new technology enterprises, the birth of the World Wide Web, the further globalization of the economy, the ever-changing political environment, and the expansion and bursting of the Internet bubble. According to them the relative importance of the most desired qualities has varied over time, but there has been no change in the fact that these are the four qualities people want most in their leaders. They said whether we believe our leaders are true to these values is another matter, but what we would like from them has remained constant. This probably might be a good explanation for the continuous leadership failures as highlighted in chapter two above. It is true that the failures reported in that chapter were all political leadership failures, but Kouze et al have confirmed that if people are to willingly follow a leader to anywhere, the leader should be trustworthy.

Principle-Centred Leadership

Covey (1992) in his work on principle-centred leadership made a strong point that leaders using manipulative strategies and tactics to get other people to do what they want, while their character are flawed or competency questionable, cannot be successful over time. He was of the opinion that rhetoric and good intentions aside, if there is little or no trust, there is no foundation for permanent success. To him trustworthiness is based on character and competence. He added that leaders or chief executives can gain the trust of their subordinates if they are competent and have character that can be trusted. The point made here about trust and trustworthiness are very much in agreement with the focus of this research and the earlier argument by Adair (1983), and Kouzes and Posner (2002) on the need for the leaders to be trustworthy so as to command the trust of the followers. Covey further argued that natural laws, based upon principles, operate regardless of our awareness of them or our obedience to them. According to him the only thing that endures over time is the law of the farm. He stated that if managers learn to manage things and lead people, they will have the best bottom line because they will unleash the energy and talent of people.

Covey argued that showing more integrity to basic principles requires that we recognize the need for change within, that great breakthroughs often represent internal breaks with traditional ways of thinking. He refers to these as paradigm shifts (Covey, 1992). His principle-centered leadership introduces a new paradigm that we center our lives and our leadership of organizations and people on certain 'true north' principles. He argued that our effectiveness is predicated upon certain inviolate principles – natural laws in the human dimension that are just as real, just as unchanging as laws such as gravity are in the physical dimension. These principles, according to him are not invented by the society, but are the laws of the universe that pertain to human relationships and human organizations. They are part of the human condition, consciousness, and conscience. He argued further that survival and stability or disintegration and destruction on the other hand depend on the degree people recognize and live in harmony with such basic principles as fairness, equity, justice, integrity, honesty, and trust. It is interesting to note that what Covey referred to as basic principles here are mainly traits (Northouse, 2001). It could therefore be further argued that leaders should possess relevant traits, especially integrity as basic or fundamental requirement for effective leadership. Other issues like style (Blake and Mouton, 1964, 1978, 1985; Fleishman, 1973; Blake and McCanse, 1991), situation (Hersey & Blanchard, 1977, 1988; Blanchard, Zigarmi, & Nelson, 1993), and contingency (Fiedler & Garcia, 1987; Fiedler & Chemers, 1974) may be taken into consideration wherever and whenever necessary.

Covey went further to say that people instinctively trust those whose personality is founded upon correct principles and that technique is relatively unimportant compared to trust, which is the result of our trustworthiness over time. This again is very much in agreement with the argument by Kouzes and Posner (2002). Covey illustrated this point with the fact that when trust is high, we communicate easily, effortlessly, instantaneously and even when there is mistakes under this condition, people will still capture our meaning, but when trust is low communication becomes difficult, ineffective, time-consuming and difficult. The issue of trust in leadership is clearly well illustrated and emphasized here like was done by Adair (1983), and Kouzes and Posner (2002). All these have shown that leaders who want to be effective should make conscious efforts to build trust that will command respect and enhance performance.

According to Covey, correct principles are like compasses, and they are always pointing the way, and apply at all time in all places. They surface in the form of values, ideas, norms, and teachings that uplift, ennoble, fulfill, empower, ad inspire people. Principle-centered leadership is based on the reality that we cannot violate these natural laws with impunity (Covey, 1992). Covey said that individuals are more effective and organizations more empowered when they are guided and governed by these proven principles, and that they are not easy, quick-fix solutions to personal and interpersonal problems. Rather, they are fundamental principles that when applied consistently become behavioral habits enabling fundamental transformations of individuals, relationships, and organizations. Covey's arguments are very supportive of the main argument of this study, and give hope that poor leadership situation in a third world country like Nigeria could be transformed by these proven principles which bother so much on integrity (Adair, 1883). According to him, principles, unlike values, are objective and external. They operate in obedience to natural laws, regardless of conditions.

Seven Habits Model – Seven Habits Of Highly Effective People

This again was developed by Stephen Covey. It is a theory that he argued is applicable to our personal, social as well as our working life, but Seven Habits framework is highly applicable for leaders and managers. According to Covey our paradigms will affect how we interact with others, which in turn will affect how they interact with us. Covey argued here that any effective self-help program must begin with an "inside-out" approach, rather than looking at our problems as "being out there". He said that we must start by examining our own character, paradigms, and motives. This again is pointing to the importance and relevance of traits (Northouse, 2001).

The seven habits as expressed by Covey are: 1) Be Proactive; 2) Begin with the end in mind; 3) Put first things first; 4) Think win-win; 5) Seek first to understand and then to be understood; 6) Synergize; and 7) Sharpen the saw. According to him, being proactive is the ability to control one's environment, rather than have it control you, as is so often the case. He said that managers need to control their own environment, using self-determination and the power to respond to various circumstances. Determination and courage are traits (Northouse, 2001). Beginning with the end in mind, he said, means that the manager needs to be able to see the desired outcome and concentrate on activities which help in achieving that end. This again could be said to be the same thing as forward-looking (Kouzes and Posner, 2002) which is a trait. He explained that putting first things first requires that the managers need to personally manage themselves and implement activities which aim to achieve the second habit – looking to the desired outcome. He said that habit (2) is the first, or mental creation; habit (3) is the second, or physical creation. Thinking win-win, to him is the most important aspect of interpersonal leadership because most achievements are based on cooperative effort, therefore the aim needs to be win-win solutions for all.

Seeking first to understand and then to be understood, according to him, requires developing and maintaining positive relationships through good communications and through this the manager can be understood, and can understand the subordinates. Synergizing, according to him is the habit of creative cooperation – the principle that collaboration often achieves more than could be achieved by individuals working independently towards attaining a purpose. Covey sees sharpening the saw as learning from previous experience and encouraging others to do the same. He sees development as one of the most important aspects in being able to cope with challenges and aspire to higher levels of ability. All these in a nut shell have a lot to do with leadership qualities and what leaders, especially organizational leaders should do to achieve results.

Positive Ratings For Integrity By Successful Ceos And Research Bodies

Northouse (2001) stated that Integrity is the quality of honesty and trustworthiness, and individuals who adhere to a strong set of principles and take responsibility for their actions are exhibiting integrity. As have been stated earlier it is a very important trait that leaders must possess in addition to courage, intelligence, foresight and knowledge. Adair (1983) as stated earlier, argued that many writers on leadership have stressed the importance of integrity, which Viscount Slim defined as "the quality which makes people trust you". Leaders with integrity inspire confidence in others because they can be trusted to do what they say they are going to do (Northouse, 2001). Kouzes and Posner (2002) said that when people talked to them about the qualities they admire in leaders, they often use "integrity" and "character" as synonymous with honesty. Honesty, strong moral principles and trustworthiness are all about integrity and could therefore be said to be desirable qualities that professional managers should possess if organizations are to be led effectively and do business with international investors, especially in an environment where dishonest and fraudulent practices had already caused some disaffection and mistrust. Cunningham T.M. (2002) stated that of all the qualities a leader must possess, integrity may be the most important one of them all. He added that integrity involves the three Rs: Respect for self; Respect for others; and Responsibility for all your actions. He went further to say that there is a common theme among experts who have studied or written about modern leadership, and the theme is that all leaders must act with integrity at all times. It is encouraging to note here that the main argument of this research is very much in agreement with the theme of modern leadership writers. Kane (2006) considered integrity and courage as attributes of leadership and stated that leaders' effectiveness is impaired when they are not sound within themselves because that soundness provides the foundation for integrity. She stated that effective and enlightened leaders live in integrity even when it is challenging. According to her leaders who operate in integrity create willingness in people to trust and follow them. Courage she said is of utmost importance in maintaining integrity. To back up her points she quoted some supportive statements on integrity from known CEOs as follows:

1. Steve Black, President, & CEO, Pathway Communities, Peachtree City, Georgia. –

"I think the number one trait is integrity. If you don't have the values then nothing else is going to happen as far as truly being a leader."

2. Ulf Peterson, President, Megadoor, Inc., Peachtree City. –

"Integrity is incredibly important and it should be in your spine. You must make sure that you don't have two sets of values, one for yourself and one for your employee."

3. L.B. "Bud" Mingledorff, President, Mingledorff's Inc., Norcross. –

"If you don't have integrity you cannot do business with companies that have integrity. I would say that as a company, having integrity is not only moral imperative, it is an immense competitive advantage. Leadership without integrity is impossible."

Adair (1983) went further to say that where there is lack of trust in working relationships it is often a symptom of a failure in personal or corporate integrity. He added that the primary meaning of integrity is wholeness, but that it also has a moral sense. According to him it suggests the type of person who adheres to some code of moral, artistic or other values and prominent among those values is the concept of truth. It can therefore be said that where there is no truth, falsehood may likely prevail, and falsehood may likely breed corruption. A nation that has abundance of corrupt managers may eventually not be trusted at international level and may not be able to attract any reasonable foreign investment. Such nation may therefore not be able to grow to its full potential and ability to compete in the global village. The long-term effects of this in such country would be poverty for the citizen. Integrity is therefore of primary importance in this research exercise, because the aim is to establish the effects of the chief executive's integrity on the subordinates as well as the organization's productivity and overall performance and growth.

Incidentally the current development in the world economy seems to be making special demand on corporate leaders, and integrity has continued to feature as a vital attribute for effective leadership. For example, Galvanek and Konczal (2005) stated that while leadership is always important to corporate performance, there is a growing realization that effective leaders with integrity are absolutely, crucial for successful navigation of the new Economy of the 21st Century. They stated that integrity is a delicate jewel, and that building integrity in leaders and their organizations takes time, continuous effort and cannot be feigned. They also stated that leaders with integrity: deliver their message clearly and do not worry about revealing themselves; must have a clear vision of who they are and what they stand for; and firmly believe that doing the right and ethical thing is the overarching way to do business. They added that the characteristics of the 21st Century leader are dramatically different from the leader of the past, even the recent past. According to them command and control is out, organizations are getting flatter, the competitive landscape is chaotic, people are looking for meaningful work, customers are in control, and more demands are being placed on today's leaders. Transition to the new economy are frequently compared to movement to the Industrial Economy, the Information Economy, but the breath of developments and changes in the New Economy are so dramatic that there is little precedent. According to them the real job of leaders is to inspire and create meaning and direction in the midst of drastic change and even chaos. In such a world of change and ambiguity, a new leadership style is needed. Galvanek and Konczal went further to emphasize the need to grasp the paradoxes inherent in the New Economy and master the competencies required by the business environment now being created. They said that the new business environment will require leaders acting as authentic and inspirational force developing effective relationships with people in the company, partners, customers, competitors and any other stakeholders.

The need for leadership with integrity seems to be gathering momentum and is being recognized gradually as a world-wide requirement. Danny Leipziger (2006) as the World Bank Vice President for Poverty Reduction and Economic Management commented on the outcome of the recent World Ethics Forum, from Washington DC, and said: "Leadership with Integrity is the missing link in the current governance discussions." He welcomed the actions identified by the forum and hope they will contribute to the global effort to foster good governance. The first World Ethics Forum on Leadership, Ethics and Integrity in public life held in Oxford in UK from 9th to 12th April, 2006, came to conclusion that corruption and poor governance around the world will only be overcome through much greater emphasis on ethics and integrity in leadership. The conclusion of the forum is again very much in agreement with the main argument of this research. Incidentally the forum brought together over 250 leaders, thinkers, development practitioners, and youth from over 70 developed and developing countries, and participants were those who have made significant contributions to improving governance in their countries, and have demonstrated exemplary leadership in the public sector, civil society, media or local communities. The forum was a powerful one and was able to make meaningful contributions to leadership knowledge. The goal was to develop, empower, and connect leaders committed to integrity at all levels and in practical ways specifically through: awareness raising, recognition, and networking; coalition building across nations and sectors, and alliances for action; capacity-building for ethical, effective leadership; and supporting emerging leaders and providing resources and refuge for existing ethical leaders. Interestingly one initiative proposed at the forum is the global Integrity Alliance (GIA), which will recognize, support and enable the formation of coalitions of leaders from different sectors of society committed to integrity. With all these developments it could be argued positively that integrity as a trait has come a long way and should now be seen and accepted as a fundamental requirement for effective leadership. In other word it could be said that organizations will work better if the people in managerial positions have designated leadership profiles (Northouse, 2001) and integrity should be considered as number one.

The National Survey By Centre For Social Science Research & Development

The report of a national survey conducted at the Centre for Social Science Research and Development (CSSR&D), Nigeria, by Agbaje, Okunola and Alarape (2003), showed also that in Nigeria, Honesty or Integrity is the most mentioned of expected leadership attributes in three of five areas commented upon in the survey, although there is diversity in expectations, just as was reported in Kouzes and Posner (2002) research, narrated earlier under section 3.4. This survey according to Agbaje et al, had a central objective of providing a basis for a better appreciation of Nigerian leadership problem by finding Nigerians' understanding, experiences and assessments of leadership, political and non-political, governmental and non-governmental, local and national, as well as their expectations and visions of the future in this regard. According to the report, the survey involved the administration of 2,600 instruments on Nigerians in 52 randomly selected settlements (26 urban, 26 rural) drawn from 13 states, selected from the country's six geo-political zones of North-central, North-east, North-west, South-east, South-south, and South-west. This survey was mainly conducted between October and November, 2002, and the follow-ups, re-checks, clarifications and re-runs were accordingly completed in December, 2002. This coincidentally was the year Kouzes and Posner (2002) completed their latest edition. The survey report also stated that in the same vein, while responses also vary from sphere to sphere, issue to issue, in terms of the final details of what they do not expect their leaders to do or be, majority of Nigerians detest dubious, corrupt or fraudulent leaders, followed by those that are not disciplined, just, objective, patient, hardworking, selfless and intelligent, among others. Based on all these it could be concluded that majority of Nigerians like their counterpart in other parts of the world,

want to be fully confident in their leaders, and to be fully confident they have to believe that their leaders are people of strong
character and solid integrity (Kouzes and Posner, 2002). This is
irrespective of the fact that Nigeria is seen as a corrupt country.

National Survey By Guardian Newspapers Ltd

Apart from the survey reported above, a Guardian Opinion Poll conducted between 2002 and 2003 and published in 2003 also showed that respondents doubt rulers' integrity. The poll asked the question "To what degree do you trust the three arms of government in Nigeria to do what is in the interest of the people?" The options available were High Degree, Moderate Degree, Low Degree and No comment for the Executive, Legislative and the Judiciary arms. The sample size of the survey was 2,800. The report stated that out of this sample size, a cumulative number of 1,135 or 40.5% rated the executive as 'Low', 33.2% Moderate, and 18% others High. While 7.1% did not comment, and invalid score stood at 1.2%. Apart from the executive, the legislature also got a 'Low Degree' rating of 1,455 or 52%, 27.7% for Moderate, High Degree of 9.4% and 'No comment' votes of 9.6. The Invalid cases of 1.4% were recorded. The Judiciary had 'Low Degree' rating of 1,129 or 40.3%. Those respondents that favoured 'Moderate Degree' got 32% and High Degree was 15.9%. 'No Comment' was 10.4% while invalid was 1.5%. The outcome of this survey seemed to have complimented the survey by CSSR&D reported above by indirectly confirming that their leaders lack integrity.

The result was given a zonal breakdown and it showed that the respondents who rated the executive on a 'Low Degree' were 51.5% in the North West, 47% in the South East and 43.5% in the South South. The North Central was 34.3%, North East 29%, and South West 27.3%. Lagos and Abuja secured 55% and 47.55% respectively. The Legislature's 'Low Degree' rating in the zones were: South West 59.8%, North West 56.8%, South South 53.8%, South East 50.5%, North Central 49.3%, and North East 36.8%. Lagos was 62% while Abuja got 52%. For the Judiciary, the 'Low Degree' rating was 46.5% for North West,

42.8% for South West, 41.3% for South South, 38% for South East, 35.5% for North Central, and 35% for North East. Lagos was 49% and Abuja got 37.5%. The overall picture painted here again, based on the statistics, is that of lack of trust (Adair, 1983) of the leadership at the three arms of government, by the citizens, due possibly to what the citizens perceived as lack of integrity in the conducts of the leaders at various arms of the government. All the three arms of government got poor ratings, and this shows that the country has got to do something about the issue of integrity if the country's leadership is to have the trust of the followers.

The summary of these survey reports could be said to be a testimony that Nigerians know what they want in their leaders and that they would likely follow trustworthy leaders (Adair, 1983) when they are selected. These reports are again pointing to the fact that the failures of leadership in Nigeria as reported in chapter four is mainly due to greed and corrupt practices (Eghagha, 2003) of the political class and the military politicians. The detailed accounts given in chapter four and the outcome of these surveys are strong evidence that the Nigerian citizens do not trust their leaders, especially the political leaders. They detest dubious, corrupt or fraudulent leaders and those that are not disciplined (Agbaje, Okunola and Alarape, 2003). It could therefore be said that the poor political leadership in Nigeria calls for shift of paradigm. Nigeria need to adopt a new approach in selecting political and other leaders since the system existing now is that of "cash and carry" leadership. This has so far produced poor results that affect other levels of leadership in the country, including organizational leadership which is the main focus of this research. The political leadership in a given context is supposed to be a model for other levels of leadership in the same context. It is therefore likely that improved political leadership and good governance will help to improve the quality of organizational leadership and others. It is expected that perhaps leaders with integrity might be the answer since it has been clearly stated that effective leadership is based on trust, and integrity according to Viscount Slim (cited in Adair, 1983), is the quality which makes people trust you.

CHAPTER THREE

Leadership And Management,
A Comparative Analysis

There is need to look at leadership and management comparatively at this point in order to appreciate the similarities and differences between the two, and to understand the complimenting roles expected from both in any given organization where effective performance is expected. The argument has so far been focused on leadership which is a process that is similar to management in many ways. Leadership as has been explained already involves influence (Bryman, 1992) and so is management to a reasonable extent. A leader can be a manager, but a manager is not necessarily a leader (Allen, 1998). The leader of the work group may emerge informally as the choice of the group. Kotter (1990) stated that managers must know how to lead as well as manage. He stated further that without leading as well as managing, today's organizations face the threat of extinction. Management is the process of setting and achieving the goals of the organization through the functions of management: planning, organizing, directing (leading), and controlling (Henri Fayol, 1916).

It is therefore clear here that management involves leading amongst other activities and Kotter (1990) was right to state that managers must know how to lead as well as manage. It could therefore be right to agree with Kotter (1990) that without leading as well as managing, today's organizations face the threat of extinction. This is more so when the argument is related to the position of the chief executive of the organization. This research is about effective leadership at organizational level and therefore has a lot to do with leading and managing. The conclusion therefore, is that the chief executive must know how to lead as well as manage, without this the organization faces the threat of extinction (Kotter, 1990). A manager is hired by the organization and is given formal authority to direct (Henri Fayol, 1916) the activities of others in fulfilling organization goals. Therefore, leading is a major part of manager's job. Despite this a manager must also plan, organize and control. It could be said that leadership deals with the interpersonal aspects of a manager's job whereas planning, organizing and controlling deal with the administrative aspects. Leadership deal with change, inspiration, motivation, and influence and management deal more with carrying out the organization's goals and maintaining equilibrium (Allen, 1998).

Leadership is concerned with effective goal accomplishment and this is equally applicable to management. Many of the functions of management enumerated above are activities that are in line with all we have so far analyzed and explained about leadership. From the historical accounts given (Bittel, Ramsey, & Bittel, 1990), management was created for the purpose of reducing the chaos in organizations and to make them more efficient and effective.

The primary functions of management as first enumerated by Fayol (1916), were planning, organizing, leading, staffing, and controlling, and these are still valid and relevant in the field of management today. Kotter (1990) tried to compare the functions of management with the functions of leadership and argued that the functions of the two are quite dissimilar. He argued that the overriding function of management is to provide order and consistency to organizations, whereas the primary function of leadership is to produce change and movement.

To him, management is about seeking order and stability, while leadership is about seeking adaptive and constructive change. Kotter's (1990) views appear to have ignored the dynamism of management. The highly competitive global market of today has kept the management on its toes and induced strategic thinking and planning for survival. It is therefore difficult to accept that the overriding function of management is just to provide order and consistency to organizations. It could be argued that management overriding function today goes beyond this, and indeed includes producing change and movement attributed to leadership. Leading outstanding organizations today create and introduce changes whenever and wherever these will enhance their profitability, growth and maintenance of leading positions. Indeed, it could be argued that for the chief executive to succeed in the organization of today, he or she needs to possess the relevant traits (Northouse, 2001) and develop strong leadership ability to produce change and movement. It is a common knowledge today that employers of labour, especially in the selection process of the chief executive of organizations would go for the candidates that exhibit great leadership potentials and traits (Kirkpatrick & Locke, 1991). The trait approach suggests that organizations will work better if the people in managerial positions have designated leadership profiles (Northouse, 2001). The successful management of organizations of today demands great leadership ability from the chief executive and foresight to identify opportunities before the competitors and to introduce the relevant changes that would move the organization forward.

Kotter also argued that in planning and budgeting, the emphasis of management is on establishing detailed agendas, setting timetables that run into months and to few years, allocating the resources to all these activities to ensure that the organizational objectives are met at the end of the period. He went further to say that in contrast to leadership, the emphasis of leadership is on direction setting, clarification of the big picture, and building vision that is mostly long-term as well as formulating strategies to create needed organizational changes. This argument is in order, in view of the fact that management has the major role of implementing the long-term goals of the organization as given in the policies formulated by the board of directors. He also looked at organizing and staffing from the management perspectives as focusing on providing structure to the work of the employees, as well as taking care of their relationships within the organization, and the physical context. For him this includes placement of workers in the right jobs, and providing rules and procedures on how work is to be done in the organization. From the leadership point of view, according to him, organizing and staffing is simply making the vision of the organization known to the employees and getting them committed so as to work with them and build the team that will ensure the accomplishment of the organization's goals. He sees the controlling and problem-solving activities from the management point of view as simply developing incentive systems to motivate the workforce, solving problems and monitoring progress toward the performance goals to ensure corrective measures on any deviation. From the leadership point of view, however, he argued that the emphasis is on motivating, inspiring, and empowering them to satisfy their outstanding needs.

Bennis and Nanus (1985), also argued that leadership and management are distinct constructs and that there is significant difference between them. From their point of view, to manage means to accomplish activities and master routines, while to lead means to influence others and create visions for change. They went further to simplify their views in their often-quoted phrase "Managers do things right and the leaders do the right thing". It could again be argued that managing is not just accomplishing activities and mastering routines. It also involves influencing others and creation of required changes within the organization in particular, and influencing external changes within the environment through external pressure on government and lobbying. Managers can also do the right thing if the organization is to remain relevant and survive on the long-term.

Rost (1991) also contended that leadership is a multidirectional influence relationship and management is a unidirectional authority relationship. He went further to explain that leadership is concerned with the process of developing mutual purposes, while management is to do with coordinating activities to ensure that the job is done. It could be argued rightly that management is getting things done. Rost added that leaders and followers work together to create real change, and that managers and subordinates join forces to sell goods and services. As stated earlier, it will be difficult to exclude managers from the creation of real change because they will always remain part of change creation. Besides the idea of managers and subordinates joining forces to sell goods and services is debatable because the claim is not universally acceptable. It is not all the organizations that are involved in the sell of goods and services. Some are indeed purely change agents and very regulatory in nature. It therefore sounds like a sweeping statement to say that leaders and followers work together to create real change, while managers and subordinates join forces to sell goods and services.

Zalenznik (1977) viewpoint was unique in a way but interesting. He argued that leaders and managers themselves are distinct, and that they are basically different types of people. He argued that managers are reactive and prefer to work with people to solve problems but do so with low emotional involvement. Here again one begins to wonder whether Zalenznik based his argument on ineffective managers or result-oriented managers. Effective managers are result-oriented and they are supposed to be proactive and very much committed and involved in what they set out to do. He suggests that leaders, on the other hand, are emotionally active and involved, and that they seek to shape ideas rather than responding to them, and have the tendency to expand the available options to any outstanding problems. He contended that leaders change the way people think about what is possible. These are very correct about effective leaders and there is no argument about these except that result-oriented managers can equally do the same whenever they focused on any given tasks. Interestingly, Marcus Buckingham (2005), in highlighting what great managers do, stated that "Great leaders tap into the needs and fears we all share. Great managers, by contrast, perform their magic by discovering, developing, and celebrating what is different about each person who works for them." This goes to support the fact that managers, especially great managers cannot easily be dismissed as just routine and reactive people. They can be very proactive.

Generally, on the comparison of leadership and management, it could be said that there are some differences between management and leadership, or between managers and leaders. It is very important, however, to point out that there is a reasonable amount of overlap. Yukl (1989) arguments were in support of this. Clearly put, when managers are involved in influencing (Bryman, 1992) a group to meet its goals, they are involved in leadership. This indeed is a regular activity of managers when they are trying to get things done. On the other hand when leaders are involved in planning, organizing, staffing, and controlling, they are involved in management. This happens quite often because leaders also plan even if it means planning for long-term goals. All these involve influencing (Bryman, 1992) a group of people towards a predetermined goal. It could therefore be said that an effective manager needs leadership ability and skills to achieve and sustain acceptable results in the organization. At the same time effective leader also needs reasonable level of management ability and skills to achieve and sustain his or her leadership success in any given organization. In line with all the above arguments it could be concluded that effective management could be enhanced with reasonable level of leadership skills and ability, while effective leadership on the other hand needs good dose of management skills and ability for sustenance. This remains the line of argument of this research because management and leadership involve influence (Bryman, 1992), and good results come by positive influence.

Modern Management

Modern management thinking came to prominence when Peter Drucker (1954) in his book, "The Practice of Management", confidently asserted that management had arrived as a distinct and a leading group in industrial society. He said then that rarely, if ever, has a new basic institution, a new leading group, emerged as fast as has management since the turn of the century. He added that rarely in human history has a new institution proved indispensable so quickly. For over fifty years later, Drucker's bold pronouncement is still holding true. Management is the art and science of our times and we are all managers today, whether we manage companies, hospitals, schools, football teams or farms. Laurie J. Mullins (1995) stated that organizations can only achieve their goals and objectives by the coordinated efforts of their members, and it is the task of management to get work done through other people. The modern management is about getting things done through and with other people within the organization.

Historical Accounts

The study of leadership can be traced back to Aristotle, while management emerged around the turn of the 20th century with the advent of our industrialized society (Northouse 2001). This shows that the study of leadership has a longer history and therefore older than the study of management. According to Peter Drucker, management both as a practice and as a field of study has a respectable history, in many different countries especially in the United States, going back almost two centuries. He therefore said that it was wrong for recent writers in management to give the impression that management is an invention of the years after the second world-war. He however, acknowledged the fact that before the world-war II, interest in, and study of management was confined to small groups. Bittel, Ramsey and Bittel (1990) historical accounts of management development given in the Encyclopedia of Professional Management, also point to the same direction. According to this account, awareness of the importance of management skills dates back beyond the beginning of written history. Most historians, however, generally date the first recognized attempts at systematically studying the development of basic management principles to the last two decades of the nineteenth century. Bittel, Ramsey, & Bittel (1990) stated that between 1910 and 1920, Scientific Management was recognized as a respectable university discipline, courses in the "new" management movement were offered at higher institutions such as Columbia University, Cornell University, Pennsylvania State University and the Massachusetts Institute of Technology. Bittel et al stated that at that time, increased interest in management was paralleled by the growing economic and industrial development of the United States and Western Europe. The forces of expanding technology and commerce, paired with new advances in transportation and communication, dramatically increased the scope and complexity of business undertakings.

The problems of managing large scale organizations became widespread and industrial and commercial enterprises began the process of replacing individual proprietors and partnerships as the usual forms of business. Subsequently the increase in the size of production facilities gave rise to the problem of waste and inefficiency. It was these problems, according to Bittel et al that necessitated formulating and investigating new concepts for the scientific management of work. This according to them is what is often referred to as the beginning of the search for a rational and systematic science of management. In line with historical account, this became pronounced in 1886 with the presentation of a paper titled "Engineer as Economist", at a meeting of the American Society of Mechanical Engineers (ASME), by Henry R. Towne, an engineer and then the president of the Yale and Towne Manufacturing Company. The paper, according to the report stressed the importance of management as a field of independent study equal to that of engineering. Towne, noting the almost complete absence of management literature, the virtual absence of a medium for the exchange of administrative ideas and experience, and the total lack of management associations, suggested that the ASME should serve as a centre for the development of an understanding of industrial management. The suggestion, according to report was considered nothing less than revolutionary.

The Birth of Scientific Management

In line with Peter Drucker's argument, way back in 1911, Frederick W. Taylor became the father of scientific management. This was because the birth of the Scientific Management Movement was to his credit. However, Henry Towne (1886) presentation is recognized as marking the beginning of the search for a science of management. Taylor (1911), in his book "The Principles of Scientific Management", questioned the traditional role of management. He conceived of management's new duties as involving:

-       Development of true science of managing complete with clearly stated laws, rules and principles to replace old   rule-of–thumb methods;

-       Scientific selection, training and development of workers   (whereas in the past workers were randomly chosen and often untrained);

-       Enthusiastic co-operation with workers to ensure that all work performed is done in accordance with scientific principles;

-       Equal division of tasks and responsibilities between the worker and management.

Believing that the interest of employers and employees could be made to coincide, Taylor was resolutely committed to eliminating the inefficient and wasteful practices of the past and to transcending what at the time appeared to be irreconcilable conflicts of interests between labour and management.

With the efforts of Taylor and other contributors the trend of management development continued and between 1910 and 1920, scientific management was recognized as a respectable university discipline, courses in the "new" management movement were offered at higher institutions such as Columbia University, Cornell University, Pennsylvania State University and Massachusetts Institute of Technology. It was reported by Bittel, Ramsey, & Bittel (1990) that the first formal assembly on management, a gathering of some 300 educators, industrialists and consultants was called in 1911 at the Amos Tuck School of Administration and Finance at Dartmouth College.

Subsequently the first professional management association came into being in 1914 with the founding of the society to promote the science of management. According to the history, this was re-established as the Taylor Society in 1916 and in 1930, it evolved into the present Society for Advancement of Management. Also the National Industrial Conference Board was started in 1916, followed by organizations such as the American Management Association in 1923.

These historical accounts have shown that it took dedication and continuous efforts of committed contributors to knowledge, for management profession to be developed. The effects of this on the economic development of the developed countries of the world cannot be over-emphasized. It is therefore hoped that this research efforts will not be in vain but will also make some positive contributions and impact on the development of effective leadership in the third world countries.

The Need for Management

All the above accounts and trends have shown that management study came into being as a result of needs due to changes in the industrial sectors. This is enough evidence that nothing is ever static, and that there will continue to be changes in the way things are done as a result of dynamism in our world. The activities in the world will therefore likely remain dynamic and change of processes will remain the answer to ensure relevance and avoid obsolescence. Management science was developed to cope with effective practice of management in organizations. It can therefore be said that although leadership knowledge and studies existed before the scientific management knowledge and practices, those behind the development of management were well aware of the existence of leadership knowledge and practice, but still recognized the need for the development of scientific management practice, because both have their unique roles as well as the complimentary roles, in the relevant situations.

The Functions of Management

Management is a generic term, and subject to many interpretations. According to Mullins, L. J. (1993, pp.365) a number of different ideas are attributed to the meaning of management and to the work of a manager. Drucker P. (1973) sees management as denoting a function, as well as the people who discharge it, a social position and authority, and also a discipline and field of study that considers management as tasks, as a discipline, and also as people. Jones, George, and Hill (2000) defined management as the planning, organizing, leading and controlling of resources to achieve organizational goals effectively and efficiently. From this definition it could be noted that management takes place within structured organizational setting and with prescribed roles.

It is directed towards aims and objectives, and the results are achieved through the efforts of other people and uses systems and procedures. It can therefore be said that management relates to all activities of the organization and is undertaken at all levels of the organization. Management is seen best, therefore, as a process common to all other functions carried out within the organization. Management is essentially an integrating activity (Mullins, L.J., 1993, pp.368). We could therefore say that the overall responsibilities of management could be seen as the attainment of the given objectives of the organization.

According to Henri Fayol (1916, cited in Jones, George & Hill, 2000), managers at all levels and in all departments, whether in small or large organizations, in profit or non-profit organizations, perform four major functions as follows:

Planning

Planning is a process that managers use to identify and select appropriate goals and courses of action. There are three steps in the planning process:

◆ ◆ ◆

Deciding Which Goals The Organization Will Pursue;

Deciding what course of action to adopt to attain those goals, and Deciding how to allocate organizational resources to attain those goals. How well managers plan, determine how effective and efficient their organization will be.

Organizing

Organizing is a process that managers use to establish a structure of working relationships, that allow organizational members to work together to achieve organizational goals. Organizing involves grouping people into departments according to the kinds of Job-specific tasks they perform.

In organizing, managers also layout the lines of authority and responsibility between different individuals and groups, and they decide how best to co-ordinate organizational resources, particularly human resources.

Leading

In leading, managers articulate a clear vision for organizational members to follow, and they energize and enable organizational members, so that they understand the part they play in achieving organizational goals. Leadership depends on the use of power, influence, vision, persuasion, and communication skills to co-ordinate the behaviours of individuals and groups, so that their activities and efforts are in harmony and to encourage employees to perform at a high level.

◆ ◆ ◆

Controlling

In controlling, managers evaluate how well an organization is achieving its goals, and take action to maintain or improve performance. Jones et al (2000 pp.10) stated that managers monitor the performance of individuals, departments, and the organization as a whole to see whether they are meeting desired performance standards.

The managerial functions stated above, are essential to a manager's job in every organization. At all levels in a managerial hierarchy, and across all departments in an organization, effective management means making decisions and managing these four activities successfully.

According to Gareth R. Jones et al (2000, pp.16), a role is a set of specific tasks that a person is expected to perform because of the position he/she holds in an organization. Based on the study of the work of five chief executives of medium to large organizations, Henry Mintzberg identified 10 specific roles that effective managers undertake (Mullins, L.J. 1993, pp.384). The ten specific roles are: 1) figure head; 2) leader; 3) liaison; 4) monitor; 5) disseminator; 6) spokesperson; 7) entrepreneur; 8) disturbance handler; 9) resource allocator; and 10) negotiator.

Mintzberg grouped the ten roles into three broad categories as: 1) inter-personal roles, made up of the first three specific roles, 2) informational roles, made up of the 4th, 5th, and 6th specific roles, and 3) decisional roles, made up of the 7th , 8th, 9th, and 10th specific roles. By way of description, managers assume the inter-personal roles in order to co-ordinate and interact with organizational members and provide direction and supervision for both employees and the organization as a whole.

The informational roles are closely associated with the tasks necessary to obtain and transmit information, while the decisional roles are closely associated with the methods managers use to plan strategy and utilize resources.

Managers assume each of these roles in order to influence (Bryman, 1992) the behaviour of individuals and groups inside and outside the organization. The people inside the organization include other managers and employees. Jones et al (2000, pp.17) described people outside the organization to include shareholders, customers, suppliers, the local community in which an organization is located, and any local or government agency that has an interest in the organization and what it does.

Managerial Skills

Jones, George & Hill, (2000, pp.21) stated that both education and experience help managers to recognize and develop the skills they need to put organizational resources to their best use. Research and experience have shown that for managers to perform their roles effectively, they require a combination of three principal types of skills namely:

- **Technical Skills;**

- **Social and Human Skills;**

- **Conceptual Skills.**

The degree or amount of these skills that a manager needs depends on his/her level in the managerial hierarchy as shown below:

Top-Level Managers;

Middle Level Managers;

Lower Level Managers.

Technical Skills

Technical skills are the job-specific knowledge and techniques that are required to perform an organizational role.The examples here include such skills as manufacturing, accounting, marketing or training skills. Managers need a range of technical skills to be effective. Technical skills are required more by lower level managers for the day-to-day operations concerned in the actual production of goods and services. They are also required by the higher level managers for the supervision and training of subordinate staff.

◆ ◆ ◆

Social And Human Skills

Social and human skills refer to inter-personal relationships in working with and through other people, and all the relevant exercise of judgment. Effective management of human resources demand good knowledge of human behaviour and good interaction with them to be able to understand their needs and expectations from the system and work out ways of helping them to meet such needs. The ability to communicate effectively and to co-ordinate and motivate people to put in their best towards the achievement of the objective of the organization is a good demonstration of social and human skills. It also involves molding individuals into a cohesive team. All these help to distinguish the effective managers from the ineffective ones. These skills are required by all levels of management, but more by the middle level managers.

◆ ◆ ◆

Conceptual Skills

Conceptual skills refer to the ability to analyse and diagnose a situation, and to distinguish between cause and effect and to conceive a relevant idea based on the objective findings and knowledge of the situation. Planning, organizing, problem-solving and decision-making require a high level of conceptual skill, as in the case of performing managerial roles discussed earlier. Top managers require more of conceptual skills than any other level of management, so much of this is expected from the chief executive of the organization because their primary responsibilities are planning and organizing. It is important to point out that effective managers need all the three kinds of skills like conceptual, social/human and technical skills. The complete absence of one can lead to serious failure. Jones, George and Hill (2000, pp.23) stated that the biggest problems facing small business owners/managers are the problems of lack of appropriate conceptual and human skills. They have the technical skills to do things for themselves but once the business start growing to a point where extra hands are employed, the small business owner's poor human and social skills will start having negative effects on the business. This simply show that someone who has the technical skills to start a new business may not necessarily know what to do to manage the venture successfully except if he is wise enough to get the professional manager to help him out or undergo some relevant trainings.

The brief summary given about management here is to highlight its importance and to emphasize the need for effective combination by the chief executives. Leadership with Integrity (Adair, 1983) plus effective management would likely give rise to good results.

CHAPTER FOUR

*REVIEW OF THE PERFORMANCE
OF THE POLITICAL LEADERSHIP IN
NIGERIA, FROM 1960 TO 2019.*

In this chapter, we will try to review the performance of all the political leaders that have ruled Nigeria right from the year of independence (1960) to 2019. This will cover both the civilians and the military leaders. The essence of this review is to give us insight into the achievements and failures of these leaders, so that we can appreciate the effect of integrity if any, in the successes or failures of these political leaders. I believe that a lot of useful lessons will be learnt from this exercise by future political leaders and other leaders alike.

It must be admitted that the failures of political leadership in Nigeria, started almost immediately after independence in 1960 due mainly to suspicion and mistrust amongst the politicians. They pretended to be united and tolerated each other when there was one common enemy – the colonial master. There should also be no pretence on the fact that the colonial master was not ready to let go because of huge economic benefits involved. The Nigerian politicians were very much in a hurry to start enjoying the dividends of freedom and therefore did not bother to thoroughly examine the problem of forceful amalgamation, cultural and social diversity imbedded in this entity called Nigeria. They assumed they will figure it out later.

The colonial masters must have been disappointed and probably decided to lay a faulty foundation that will make unity in diversity very difficult. The political structure that was handed over was loaded with a lot of conflicts and booby traps that started rearing its ugly heads right from the onset.

Two years down the road under the leadership of the Prime Minister, Right Honourable Sir Abubakar Tafawa Balewa, serious political mistrust and the crisis of the Action Group started at the party's annual convention held in Jos, in January 1962. At the convention, the then leader of the party, Chief Obafemi Awolowo was on one side and the Premier of Western Nigeria at that time, Chief Samuel Ladoke Akintola, was on the other side. One will not fail to wonder why there should be such conflict between two yoruba political leaders that had been working together all along. We may not be able to give comprehensive answer here but rather suspect that there was mistrust and human greed at work. The issue of integrity in leadership, started almost immediately to manifest. This crisis escalated in Western Nigeria where political thuggery and destruction of lives and properties became the order of the day and subsequently led to the first military coup in January 15, 1966 by five young ambitious Majors in the Nigerian army.

These Majors were inexperienced in politics and did not appreciate the ethnic complexities of the nation. They were in a hurry to fix the Nigerian problem without proper analysis and knowledge in political leadership. They were anxious to bring sanity to the violent situation when the Federal government failed to do so, because of mistrust and accusation for vested interest in escalation of the conflicts. These young men were trained to be soldiers, and were meant to protect the territorial integrity of the nation and fight wars where there are any. They were not politicians and had no right to take the lives of fellow citizens for any flimsy excuses. When they struck, they killed most of the Nigerian political leaders at that time, without the involvement of any ethnic group. They wrongly thought that they were doing a good job for Nigeria. Their actions did not solve any political leadership problem in Nigeria. Instead it made the situation worse, and made innocent Ibo ethnic group that were enjoying peace in their own region to be roped in and massacred for no fault of theirs, while the originators of this conflict made a huge gain out of the very bad situation that developed. Initially the coup plotters actions were greeted with jubilation all over the country until ethnic interpretation was unfortunately given to the coup.

The January 15, 1966 coup led to the counter coup of the same year, and numerous other coups by the same military. The innocent Ibos paid dearly for the action of the few military men who did not even consult them as an ethnic people before their action. The Ibos were murdered all over the nation. They paid the supreme price for what they did not do. This was a sad moment in the history of political leadership in Nigeria. The big politicians were selfishly struggling for power and fame and their actions and inactions subsequently caused the death of innocent people. It was a big failure of political leadership in Nigeria and there was no apology. It was genocide, it was painful and was unfair treatment to the victims. The political crisis in Western Nigeria was the genesis of the coup and subsequently the civil war which consumed additional three million Ibos between May 1967 and January 1970.

The lesson of political leadership has been learnt here that one group within the system can spark off conflicts that may go beyond them and consume innocent groups outside. It is imperative to learn from this failure that our political leaders lack the ability to critically analyse and trace problems to its source for effective solution. Nigerian politicians have a flare for a cut and nail solution or better still, a tendency to supress the truth and get carried away by false propaganda. Political leaders in Nigeria must learn to leave the seat of power when their time is up and should avoid actions that may waste the lives of innocent citizens. Politicians must learn to be servant leaders and avoid the usage of thugs in achieving their aims through shedding of blood. We have no ability to give life to any one and so we should not take anybody's life no matter the status. The sit tight mentality or perpetuity in political office in Africa and in Nigeria must be abolished if we are to make head way in Africa. The political conflicts in Western Nigeria between the two top leaders of the same political party and same ethnic group can easily be traced to power struggle. The political conflict was not dealt with appropriately and on time, and it escalated to consume innocent citizens, including the first Prime Minister of Nigeria in January 1966.

We saw deterioration of political leadership in Nigeria in the hands of the military, because they left the profession for which they were trained to forcefully grab the political leadership they were not prepared for. They made several promises they could not keep because of lack of ability.

The first Nigerian Prime Minister, Sir Abubakar Tafawa Balewa was a fine gentleman but he did not have a peaceful and conducive atmosphere to fully demonstrate his political leadership ability. The political leadership capability has further deteriorated, and corruption has grown in Nigeria, from the original small scale to a monster. It is disappointing to note that more than ten years after the author's report on the political leaders' performance as analysed in his thesis submitted and defended at the University of Manchester, in 2007, no improvement has been recorded in political leadership. The only difference is that three additional heads of state have been added to the list, from 2007 to 2019. The third is still in office. He completed his first term of four years in office in May, 2019. He had started the second term since then. He was once a military head of state from 1983 to 1985. In view of the foregoing, we will at this point look at the performances of the Nigerian political leaders as earlier presented and an update would be added for those who joined the ranks from 2007.

Nigerian International Biography Centre (1999) stated that Sir Tafawa Balewa was born in 1912 in Tafawa Balewa, Bauchi State and was assassinated on January 15, 1966 in the first coup d'etat. The Biography Centre also stated that he attended Bauchi Provincial School; Katsina Higher College, and the Institute of Education, University of London. According to this account, he returned from London and went straight into politics, and was actively involved in the then 'Bauchi Discussion Circle' which discussed issues of African concern. The biography report added that he was a member of the first Northern House of Representative, from where he was elected to the Nigerian Legislative Council in Lagos, from 1946. He was Minister of Works in 1952 and two years later he became the Minister of Transport.

According to the Nigerian International Biography Centre (1999) Nigeria got her independence in October 1960, from Britain, and the leadership fell on Sir Tafawa Balewa, who was of the Northern Peoples' Congress. The Centre reported that he became the first Prime Minister of Nigeria based on the coalition of the Northern Peoples' Congress (NPC) and the National Council of Nigeria and the Cameroons (NCNC). According to the Centre, Dr Nnamdi Azikiwe of NCNC became the ceremonial Governor-General which later changed to ceremonial President. Sir Tafawa Balewa's leadership was a civilian leadership that lasted up to 1966 and was terminated by the first military coup in Nigeria. This leadership faced all sorts of difficulties, especially the issues of unity and lack of co-operation from the other ethnic leaders, right from the onset. Eventually the political leader from the Western Nigeria, Chief Obafemi Awolowo, was convicted for treason and imprisoned, and he remained in prison until the military counter coup of July, 1966.

Ademoyega (1981) stated that the reason for the sacking of the civilian government was because economic, social, educational and political problems were not solved and corruption was rife and nepotism was the order of the day. Whether these reasons were right or wrong, the facts would remain that the coup plotters introduced a new dimension and compounded Nigerian political problems by introducing military style of dictatorship into the unstable democratic system. They succeeded in changing the course of Nigerian history for the worse. They came in to solve a political and leadership problem with military might, but they failed because they became more corrupt than the civilians they sacked. The evidence can be seen in the series of coups and counter coups that followed, and in all, corruption was always given as one of the main reasons for the putsches.

Nigerian International Biography Centre (1999) also stated that General Aguiyi-Ironsi was born in March 1924, in Umuahia, Abia State, and that he was assassinated in a military counter-coup on July 29, 1966. His early education according to the Centre was partly in the Eastern Region and later in Kano. The Biography Centre also stated that he enlisted in the Nigerian Army as a private in 1942, and rose to the rank of company Sergeant Major, in 1948, and that he went on training to Camberley Staff College in England, and was promoted to Second Lieutenant of the Royal West African Frontier Force. It was further stated that he served at Accra Ghana, before his posting to Lagos, and that he was promoted to Captain in 1953 and Major in 1955. This same source stated that he served as Equerry to Queen Elizabeth II during the Royal's visit to Nigeria in 1956, and that he was promoted Lieutenant-Colonel in 1960, and appointed Commander of the 5th Battalion in Kano. The International Biography (1999) also confirmed that he led the Nigerian contingent of the United Nation's force in the Congo and it was reported that he displayed considerable valour. Aguiyi-Ironsi, according to the Biography Centre, was, between 1961 and 1962, the military attaché to the Nigeria High Commission, London, and he received his promotion to the rank of Brigadier and returned to the Congo in 1964 after a course at the Imperial Defence College. It was reported that he was made the Commander of the entire UN Peace-Keeping Force, and that he returned to Nigeria in 1965, and was promoted Major-General, and head of the Nigerian Army. The International Biography Centre (1999) stated that the first military intervention on January 15, 1966, led by five majors in Nigerian Army, was what gave rise to leadership of the country falling on the shoulders of Major General J.T.U. Aguiyi-Ironsi.

His leadership lasted for only six months, from January, 1966 to July, 1966. The Biography Centre reported that he was killed in a counter-coup in Ibadan, while he was on a state visit to the Western Nigeria, and that he was killed along with his host, Lt Col. Fajuyi, the then military governor of Western Nigeria, who was described as a courageous soldier and a faithful subordinate of General Aguiyi-Ironsi. According to the report, Auiyi-Ironsi's regime was overthrown, and another military leader in the person of Lt Colonel Yakubu Gowon, who was his subordinate in his Lagos office, was installed as a military head of state. General Aguiyi-Ironsi's government did not achieve much or make any significant impact on the polity except the universal declaration. He was the first indigenous general in the Nigerian army who took over command from the colonial masters after the independence.

It can be said that he was not prepared for the great challenge of political leadership trusted on him unexpectedly by the radical actions of the five Majors. He was not part of the military coup as evidenced by his efforts to keep the country united. He was only trained as a soldier and was politically uninformed and highly detribalised. This was why he surrounded himself mainly with northern officers without fear that he might easily be overthrown by them and Yakubu Gowon was his right-hand man, the chief of staff. He was eventually overthrown and killed by those he trusted and depended on for his security. The result of his leadership was very strong evidence that one might be a very successful soldier but may not necessarily be a successful political leader, because the two set-ups are not the same and therefore require varying skills. Stogdill (1948) had argued that the traits that leaders possess must be relevant to situations in which the leader is functioning, and that leaders in one situation may not necessarily be leaders in another situation. This argument may have offered some explanation on why General Ironsi who was a very gallant and successful soldier could not offer effective political leadership in Nigeria after the military coup. His biography shows that he did not have adequate political leadership training and therefore had not adequate skills in political leadership. He was still learning the ropes when his opponents struck and took his life and overthrew his government. His exit can be said to have accelerated the beginning of the destruction of the military discipline, order, and command.

The Nigerian political leadership problem was further compounded after his overthrow. There were series of coups and counter-coups in Nigeria thereafter, and most of the military governments that came to power could not offer Nigeria good leadership void of corruption, mismanagement and what Eghagha (2003) called self-aggrandizement and oppression. Chief Olusegun Obasanjo, a former military head of state, and the civilian head of state, in his inaugural speech (1999), quoted that one of the greatest tragedies of military rule in recent times is that corruption, was allowed to grow unchallenged, and unchecked, even when it was glaring for everybody to see. According to him, the rules and regulations for doing official business were deliberately ignored, set aside or bye-passed to facilitate corrupt practices. If this came from a former military head of state himself, then it should not be doubted that the military governments in Nigeria did not solve the problem of corruption in Nigeria, but theirs was corrupt leadership too. Instead they allowed corruption to grow unchallenged, unchecked, the rules and regulations for doing official business were deliberately ignored, set aside or bye-passed to facilitate corrupt practices (Obasanjo, 1999). This point is argued further below to prove that the poor political leadership offered by both the civilian and the military have serious impact on the organizational leadership in Nigeria.

The Nigerian International Biography Centre (1999) reported that Gowon was born on the 19th October 1934, at Lur, Pankshin, Plateau State. He got married to Victoria Hansatu and they have one son and two daughters. Gowon also confirmed his paternity of a son known as Musa Jack Ngonadi, he had before this marriage from an Ibo lady known as Edith Ike-Okongwu, from Aro-Ndikelionwu in Orumba, Anambra State. According to Premium Times Nigeria, Musa returned to Nigeria on January 1, 2016, after the US Immigration officials deported him.   The Centre stated that Yakubu Gowon had his elementary education at St Bartholomew's School, Wusasa, Zaria, from 1939 to 1949, and that he also went to Government College, Zaria, (now Barewa College) from 1950 to 1953. It reported that he enlisted in the Nigerian Army in May 1954, and that he went to the Officer Cadet Training School Teshie, Ghana, in 1954, and Eaton Hall Chester, England, 1955, and that he was at the Royal Military Academy, Sandhurst, England, from 1955 to 1956. He was the adjutant, 4th Batallion, from 1960 to 1961. He was with UN Peace Keeping Force, Congo, 1960 to 1961. The Biography Centre reported that he was promoted Major in 1962, and Lieutenant Colonel in 1963, and that he became Adjutant-General, Nigerian Army, from 1963 to 1965. Gowon, according to the report, became the Chief of Staff, Nigeria Army, January, 1966 and member, Federal Executive Council and Supreme Military Council, from January to July, 1966. The report added that he was promoted Major-General at the start of the civil war, in June 1967, and that he became the Head of Federal Military Government and Commander-in-Chief of the Armed Forces, Federal Republic of Nigeria, after the overthrow of General Aguiyi Ironsi, from 1966 to 1975, and was promoted a full General after the end of the war in 1971.

Gowon must have learnt some lessons from the political leadership failures of his former boss and predecessor in office. He made good use of the skills of the experienced politicians. For example, he released Chief Obafemi Awolowo from prison and made him a member of his cabinet as Finance Minister. He successfully led the country throughout the war years and succeeded in keeping the country as one. He was wise enough to employ good and experienced politicians who really helped him very much in the political leadership throughout the war. He created twelve states out of the former four regions of Nigeria, and appointed governors for these states and that was a master stroke politically. The governors reported to him as the chief executive.

It could be said that his failures started after the civil war when the country experienced economic boom due mainly to increased oil exploration, exploitation and exportation (CBN, 1971). This period was indeed the period the country was destined for economic greatness, due to oil boom, as confirmed by the economic indices shown in some statistical tables. Corruptions and mismanagement of resources were the major setback during his leadership, and this was one of the reasons given for his overthrow by Murtala (1975), as confirmed by Obasanjo (1999) and so the country missed the opportunity for economic growth and greatness. He had enough resources to take the country to a greater height during the oil boom but that opportunity was lost unfortunately, otherwise the poverty level (UNDP. 2000/2001) in the country should not have been there. It can therefore be argued that he lacked the vision then and Nigeria is today paying heavily for the inactions and failures of those years.

The country is today associated with debt burden and poverty (UNDP, 2000/2001) when some few years ago the country's problem was not how to make money but how to spend it. Part of Gowon's failures was his inability to conduct democratic elections to hand over power to the civilians. He stayed in office as head of state for nine years and corruption was at a great height. David Jemibewon (1978), in confirmation of this, stated that corruption had reached such a pitch that top public functionaries wallowing in it did not bother to take the trouble to conceal the acts of their corruption from public gaze. According to him there were public outcries against some Federal Commissioners but Gowon was either unable or unwilling to act. He seemed to be enjoying the power so much that he failed to realize that the essential strategy of leadership is mobilizing power to articulate and realize the motives and goals of followers (Burns, 1978). General Gowon was eventually removed by the military coup of July 29, 1975 (Nigerian International Biography Centre, 1999), and General Murtala Mohammed came to power, as the new military head of state.

Fourth Head Of State, 1975 General Murtala Mohammed (D)

According to the Nigerian International Biography Centre (1999), General Murtala Mohammed was born on the 8th November, 1938 in Kano and died on the 13th February, 1976. The centre reported that he attended the Cikin Gida and Gidan Makama Primary Schools, Kano, and that he moved in to Government College, Zaria, and after this he enlisted in the Nigerian Army. It was also stated by the Centre that he was trained at Sandhurst Royal Academy and was posted thereafter to Army Signals, England. He was a member of the Nigerian contingent to the UN Peace-keeping Force in the Congo. According to the report, in 1963, he was put in charge of the First Brigade Signal Troop, Kaduna. He later returned to Catterick for further training. The Army posted him to One Signal Squadron, Apapa, as Commanding Officer; acting Chief Signals Officer in November 1965. The centre also reported that he was then promoted to Lieutenant-Colonel and appointed Inspector of Signals, based in Lagos, and during the civil war he commanded the then newly created Second Infantry Division. The report had it that he fought gallantly during the civil war in Nigeria, and that at the end of the war he went to the Joint Services Staff College, England. He was later promoted Brigadier and was appointed Commissioner for Communication, August 1974, under General Gowon's administration. Nigerian International Biography Centre (1999) reported that Murtala became the military Head of State and Commander-in-Chief of the Armed Forces of Nigeria on July 29, 1975, after the overthrow of the government of General Yakubu Gowon. His tenure in government was eventful but short-lived for he was assassinated in the course of a failed coup against his regime on the 13th February 1976, but before then he had initiated the creation of a new Federal Capital Territory in Abuja (Nigerian International Biography Centre, 1999).

In his maiden address to the nation, Murtala (1975) blamed Gowon for the drifting of the nation, corruption and mismanagement. It is interesting to note that Gowon was the first military head of state to be blamed for corruption. Most of the properties acquired through corruption and fraud by political leaders at different levels of government were seized from the state governors, ministers, and other top government officials who served under Gowon. The corrupt governors, ministers and others who served under Gowon were charged, tried and convicted through the various tribunals set up to try them, and the properties acquired through corruption were confiscated and converted to government properties by the Murtala's regime (Official Gazettes, 1975). General Murtala Mohammed exhibited some measure of political leadership ability. He tried hard and radically to fight corruption within six months. He achieved some measure of success and most Nigerians cherished his leadership because of the way he fought rampant corruption effectively within six months. Justice Aguda (1998) in line with this same feeling said that Nigerians were sliding little by little into the abyss of corruption, and of course, indiscipline when by pure fortune, Murtala Muhammed came to head the country.

However, according to Aguda (1998), he allowed himself to be led astray into errors which could have been avoided. He dismissed many public servants from service and terminated the appointment of many without giving them opportunity to defend themselves. The point Justice Aguda was making was that rules of natural justice should have been allowed to apply. His argument was not a defence of the performance of the dismissed civil servants, but argument for the due process of law.

Whatever the case may be, that mass dismissal introduced fear of uncertainty and lack of job security in Nigerian civil service and this seemed to have introduced another round of corruption within the civil service. The result of the uncertainty and the insecurity of jobs that the mass dismissal caused, could be said to have encouraged some civil servants to devise means of corrupt enrichment, early enough, to ensure that they would not be impoverished if and when the purge comes.

Corruption has therefore continued to manifest in the public services despite the purge by Murtala and this can be said to be a major obstacle to meaningful development in Nigeria. Despite the courageous leadership of General Murtala, he was assassinated during a failed military coup on February 13, 1976 (Nigerian International Biography Centre, 1999). This act again was a manifestation of greed, corruption and selfish ambition within the politicized Nigerian army that claimed to be corrective in action.

Fifth Head Of State, 1976
General O. Obasanjo (RTD)

The Nigerian International Biography Centre (1999) reported that General Obasanjo was born on 5th May 1937, in Abeokuta, and that he attended Baptist High School, Abeokuta. The report also had it that he went to Mons Officer Cadets School; Royal Engineers Young Officers Course, Shrivenham, England; Indian Staff College, 1965, and Royal College of Defence Studies, London, 1973 to 1974. General Obasanjo was General Officer Commanding 3rd Marine Commando Div., Nigerian army, from 1969 to 1973. He became Murtala's second in command from July 1975 to February 1976, and then the Head of State and Commander in Chief of the Federal Republic of Nigeria, after the assassination of General Murtala Mohammed in February, 1976. He tried faithfully to carry out the disengagement of military from political leadership which Murtala had mapped out before he was assassinated in 1976.

It is on record that he successfully handed power over to Al-haji Shehu Shagari as the Executive President of Nigeria in 1979 after the re-introduction of party politics in Nigeria (Nigerian International Biography Centre, 1999). The ability to hand over the power from the military back to the civilian was considered as a land mark achievement for him. This singular act earned him a great respect and trust from the international communities. Shagari contested under the National Party of Nigeria (NPN), which was regarded as a northern party. He defeated the well- known and the older political leaders like Dr Azikiwe from the east and Chief Awolowo from the west. General Obasanjo was able to hand over power to Alhaji Shehu Shagari (D) as the elected civilian president in 1979 despite all the protests.

Sixth Head Of State, 1979 Alhaji
Shehu Shagari (D)

According to the Nigerian International Biography Centre (1999), Alhaji Shehu Shagari was born on May, 1925, in Shagari Village, Sokoto. He got married to Amina Bano in 1945 and they have three sons and three daughters. It was reported that he was educated at Yabo Elementary School, from 1931 to 1935, and Sokoto Middle School, from 1930 to 1940. He went to Kaduna College from 1941 to 1944, and to the Teacher Training College, Zaria, from 1944 to 1945. He became a teacher at the Sokoto Middle School, from 1945 to 1950. The report has it that he became the headmaster of Argungu Senior Primary School, from 1951 to 1952, and became a Senior Visiting Teacher, Sokoto Province, from 1953 to 1956. The Biography Centre reported that he was elected member, House of Representative for Sokoto West from 1954 to 1956, and became Parliament Secretary to the Prime Minister from 1958 to 1959, and Acting Federal Minister, Commerce and Industries in 1958. He became the Federal Minister of Internal Affairs, from 1962 to 1965, and Federal Minister of Works, from 1965 to 1966. He was the Secretary, Sokoto Province Education Development Fund, from 1967 to 1968. He became the Commissioner for Establishment, North Western State from 1968 to 1969. The report had it that he got back to the Federal Level and became the Federal Commissioner for Economic Development, Rehabilitation and Reconstruction, from 1970 to 1971, and Federal Commissioner for Finance, from 1971 to 1975. He became the Chairman, Peugeot Automobile Nigeria Ltd, and member, Constituent Assembly, from 1977 to 1978. He was elected President, Republic of Nigeria 1979.

He was sworn in as President in 1979, despite protest and court actions especially by Chief Awolowo. It was like the resumption of old order of politics with mistrust. Some of his political opponents especially Chief Awolowo from the west, felt that his election did not conform with constitutional and statutory provisions. He carried on with the leadership despite the protest, and completed his first tenure of four years in 1983. However, sooner than later, complaints and accusation by the political opponents, of corruption were all over the country. These continued throughout his first term that ended in 1983, after four years. It is interesting to note that he survived the first term despite all the agitations by political opponents and was selected again to contest the election on the platform of NPN for the second term.

Shagari was again, declared the winner and he went ahead to form his government despite the accusations and counter accusations. The economic performance can be said to be poor and was nose-diving, and the debt burden from IMF and World Bank were on the increase, as clearly shown by the statistical indices. General Buhari (1984, cited in Rosaline Odeh, 1984) described Shagari's leadership as corrupt, inept and insensitive leadership that has been the source of immorality and impropriety in the society. He started his second term in October, 1983, and continued until the military struck and seized power on the 30th of December, 1983 (Nigerian International Biography Centre, 1999), and that marked the end of the second republic controlled by the civilians. From all the evidence and comments against this leadership, it could be said that this leadership might have contributed to the existing problems and might be classified amongst those that Eghagha (2003) said had failed the Nigerian people.

❖ ❖ ❖

The Nigerian International Biography Centre (1999) also reported that General Buhari was born on December 17, 1942, in Daura, Kaduna State, and got married to Safinatu Yusuf and they have children. It was also reported that he was educated at the Primary Schools at Daura and Mai'adua, and also went to Katsina Middle School, from 1953 to 1956. He was at Katsina Provincial Secondary School, from 1960 to 1962. The report also had it that he went to Military Training College, Kaduna; Moors Officers' Cadet School, Aldershot, England; Defence Service Staff College, Wellington, India, from 1972 to 1973. He became Director, Supply and Transport, Nigeria Army, from 1974 to 1975. The Centre also reported that he was made the Military Governor, North-Eastern State, from 1975 to 1976, and the Military Governor of Borno State in 1976. He became the Federal Commissioner for Petroleum Resources, from 1976 to 1978, and Chairman, Nigerian National Petroleum Corporation, from 1976 to 1979. The Biography Centre also reported that Buhari returned to Army duties, in July 1980 and was appointed General Officer Commanding 4 Division. It also reported that General Mohammed Buhari came to power on the 30th of December 1983, after the overthrow of Shagari government, and became Nigeria's 7th Head of State, and General Tunde Idiagbon was his deputy (Nigerian International Biography Centre, 1999). He was Head of State and Commander of the Armed Forces of the Federal Republic of Nigeria from January 1984 to August 1985.

Odeh Rosaline (1984) reported that Buhari stated that military rule in Nigeria has come to be a necessity. Civilians, according to Buhari, easily become hostage to interests that do not go hand-in-hand with the national interest. This is an interesting and debatable argument from a Nigerian military head of state. From the various accounts so far given here about coups and counter coups by the military in Nigeria, one may as well argue that some of the military coups in Nigeria were motivated by self-ambition. It could therefore be argued here that the military also easily became hostage to interests that do not go hand-in-hand with the national interest. From the reviews of the past Nigerian national leaders so far it could be said that both military and civilian leaders seemed to have failed to offer effective leadership in Nigeria. Rather than use power as a tool to transform the society they have opted to appropriate power as a vehicle for self- aggrandizement and oppression (Eghagha, 2003).

General Buhari and his deputy nevertheless, made serious efforts to provide some political leadership. They waged serious war against indiscipline (WAI) and corruption in Nigeria, and Nigerians would always remember them for the WAI. Umaru Dikko, one of the Shagari's ministers who escaped to London after the collapse of Shagari government, would always be remembered for his ordeal in the hands of Buhari/Idiagbon regime. An attempt was made to forcefully fly him from London back to Nigeria to face the charges of corruption. Buhari's regime gave some fight to corruption in Nigeria but could not defeat it. The fifty- three suit cases that were given express clearance at the Ikeja International airport, during his regime raised some doubts on issue of integrity and ability to be fair to all. He kept the overthrown president Shehu Shagari under house arrest in Ikoyi but sent the Vice president, Dr Alex Ekwueme, an Ibo man to Kirikiri maximum prison. Some of the decrees promulgated during his tenure were reported to be too draconian by the press.

The Buhari regime was terminated by a counter coup led by Babangida and Abacha on the 27th of August, 1985, after barely twenty months in office (Nigerian International Biography

Centre, 1999). Buhari did not lead the country long enough for effective assessment of his leadership. However, apart from the draconian laws, the Nigerian people seemed to have appreciated the discipline introduced within the society and the fight against the notable corrupt leaders, and this agrees with Burns (1978) suggestion that leadership is a process of morality to the extent that leaders engage with followers, on the basis of shared values, motives and goals.

◆ ◆ ◆

Eight Head of State, 1985   General I.B. Babangida (RTD)

According to the Nigerian International Biography Centre (1999), General Babangida was born on the 17th of August 1941, in Minna, Niger State, and got married to Maryam King in 1969 and had two sons and two daughters. The Centre also reported that he had his secondary education at Government College, Bida, in Niger State, from 1957 to 1962, and was trained at the Nigerian Military Training College, Kaduna, from 1962 to 1963. He was also trained at the Indian Military Academy in 1964, and at the Royal Armoured Centre UK, from 1966 to 1967. The Biography Centre also stated that he went to the Advanced Armoured School, U.S.A., from 1972 to 1973, and that he also went to the Command and Staff College, Jaji, in 1977, and to the Nigerian Institute for Policy and Strategic Study, Kuru, near Jos, in 1979. It also reported that Babangida attended the Senior International Defence Management Course, Naval Postgraduate School, U.S.A., in 1980.

The Nigerian International Biography Centre (1999) also stated that Babangida started his career as a commissioned 2nd Lieutenant, in Nigerian Army, in 1963, and was later appointed the commanding officer, 1st Reconnaissance Squadron, from 1964 to 1966. It was also reported that he was promoted to full lieutenant in 1966, and became commander, 44 Infantry Battalion (The Rangers) in 1968. He was promoted to Captain in August 1968, and later to Major in April 1970. The Centre reported that he later became Instructor and Company Commander, Nigerian Defence Academy, from 1970 to 1972. He was appointed commander, 4 Reconnaissance Regiment and was promoted Lieutenant Colonel, 1974. The report also had it that Babangida became Inspector and later Commander, Nigerian Army Armoured Corps, 1975, and that between 1977 and

1979, he was promoted to Brigadier, and in 1979 he was appointed director, Army Staff Duties and Plans. The Nigerian International Biography Centre (1999) also reported that he was promoted to Major General in March 1983, and was appointed Chief of Army Staff in December 31, 1983, and was a member of the defunct Supreme Military Council, from August 1, 1975 to 1979, and from December 1983 to 1985. The Centre also reported that Babangida became the 8th Nigerian Head of State, and Commander-in-Chief of the Armed Forces from August 27, 1985, after seizing power from General Buhari. According to the report he also became Chairman Armed Forces Ruling Council (AFRC), from August 27, 1985 to August 23, 1993, and was promoted to full General, Nigerian Army in October 1, 1987.

He provided leadership for Nigeria for 8 years within which there were series of failed coups, some of which were bloody. Many of these unsuccessful coup plotters were executed by the firing squad of the government (Armed Forces Ruling Council, Press Release, 1986). He finally stepped aside from leadership of the country, on August 26, 1993, without handing over to an elected democratic leader despite several promises to conduct election and hand over to elected civilian government. General Babangida annulled the results of the June 12, 1993 general election, on June 23, 1993 (Armed Forces Ruling Council, Press Release, 1993). He handed power over to a caretaker government headed by Ernest Shonekan rather than M.K.O. Abiola, the presumed winner of the June 12, 1993, election, considered to be the best and free election in Nigeria (Aguda, 1998). Before stepping aside, he retired most of the senior army officers that worked with him as top government officials, but General Sani Abacha was not retired (Armed Forces Ruling Council, Press Release, 1993). It is very interesting to note that it was General Sani Abacha, who later took over power from Ernest Shonekan and became a very powerful military dictator from November 1993 to June, 1998 when it was announced (Armed Forces Ruling Council, Press Release, 1998) that he died in office.

Babangida's regime brought a lot of economic hardship on the common Nigerians with the introduction of the Structural Adjustment Program (SAP) in 1986. This was the standard IMF-World Bank adjustment measure for economies that have been badly managed and therefore facing internal and external imbalances. He devalued the Nigerian currency (CBN, 1986) without attracting any serious economic benefits to the country because as shown by statistics there was nothing like increase in the exports of non-oil products (Federal Office of Statistics, 1987) as expected. There were no complimentary increases in the earnings of the working people to compensate for the devaluation, and this seemed to have fuelled poverty the more as shown on the statistical records. This period actually marked the beginning of a serious upsurge in poverty level in Nigeria. The earnings of the workers were worth little or nothing at the global market where the market forces were in action. The Nigerian GDP speaks for itself. In addition to these, the debt burden, were on the increase (CBN, 1987) and the SAP did not achieve the desired results mainly because there were a lot of inconsistencies in the application. The GDP in 1987 actually shrank by a real rate of 0.6%. Besides, no serious efforts were made to promote agriculture and the exports of the non-oil products, and oil remained the only major source of foreign exchange earnings for the country. During the SAP years, inflation rose steadily from 5.4% in 1986, to 38% in 1988, and then to 50% in 1993 (Federal Office of Statistics, 1993).

It was during Babangida's regime that Nigeria made a lot of money out of the oil wind-fall as a result of the gulf war in 1989, and there was no proper account for $12.4 billion. The Okigbo Panel Report (1994), produced by the committee set up by the Government and headed by the late economist, Dr Pius Okigbo indicted Babangida when it came out with "a gross abuse of public trust" judgement. Okigbo stated that, "had these resources of $12.4 billions, or even only a significant portion been paid into the external reserves, the impact on the naira/dollar exchange rate and the credibility of Nigeria and/or the environment for foreign investment would have been incalculable." He added that Babangida frittered that money on "what could neither be adjudged genuine projects nor truly regenerative investment." This was not denied by the government, neither was there any action taken against Babangida about this till date.

Babangida's leadership was one of the longest military dictatorship in political leadership in Nigeria (from 1985 to 1993). He made several unfulfilled promises to conduct election and hand over power to democratic leadership, and these unreliable promises eventually earned him the nickname of "Maradona" from the Nigerian press and the public. It can therefore be said that in view of all the problems and difficulties enumerated above, especially poor economic performance and increase in corruption and lack of accountability as stated by the Okigbo Panel report (1994), Babangida's leadership has contributed to the poor leadership development in Nigeria.

The trait approach to leadership (Northouse 2001) argues that organization will work better if the people in managerial positions have designated leadership profiles. It could therefore be argued that General Babangida, despite the good military background and training as stated in the biography above, may not have possessed the integrity needed for effective leadership of a nation in dire need of a trustworthy leader. It could be said that he did not sustain the fight against corruption embarked upon by General Buhari who he seized power from, instead he relaxed the measures put in place by Buhari and this subsequently promoted corruption even at official level as revealed by Okigbo Panel Report (1994).

◆ ◆ ◆

The Ninth Head Of State,
1993   Chief Ernest Shonekan

According to the Nigerian International Biography Centre (1999) Chief Shonekan was born on May 9, 1936, and completed his secondary school education in CMS Grammar School, Lagos in 1956. The Nigerian International Biography Centre also had it that in 1956 Shonekan worked in the Public Works Department (now the Federal Ministry of Works). He obtained LL.B Hons London and BL (Middle Temple). The report stated that Shonekan was called to the English Bar by the Inns Court, 1962, and was called to the Nigeria Bar in 1963. The Centre reported that he joined UAC as a Legal Assistant (Conveyancer) in 1964, and that in 1967 he had a short spell in G.B. Ollivant, a division of UAC and Nigeria Breweries Ltd, an associate company where he gained an insight into the management of industries and commercial concerns. According to the report he became the Asst. Legal Adviser later in 1967, and was promoted to Deputy Legal Adviser in 1974. It also reported that in 1975, he became a member of the Board of UAC Nigeria Ltd, and he became the General Manager, Bordpark Premier Packaging in 1978, and he became the Chairman/Managing Director, of UAC Nigeria Ltd, from 1980 to 1993.

According to the Nigerian International Biography Centre (1999) Chief Ernest Shonekan was installed as the head of the Interim government by General Babangida when he stepped aside on 26th August, 1993. He acted as the head of the Interim National Government until he was sacked by General Abacha in November 1993. The three months period was a period of uncertainty without much political leadership activities. It is therefore very difficult for any meaningful assessment to be made of this very short period. General Abacha sacked Shonekan and took over as the head of state on November 17, 1993.

Shonekan's leadership was short-lived and could not make any reasonable impact on development on the national leadership in the country, even though he has a good management and leadership background as highlighted above.

◆ ◆ ◆

General Abacha was born on the 20th of September 1943 in Kano, Kano State, and was educated at the City Senior Primary School, and the Provincial Secondary School (now Government College) in Kano between 1957 and 1962 (Nigerian International Biography Centre, 1999). The Centre also reported that thereafter he plunged into a professional career in the army, and attended the Nigerian Military Training College, Kaduna, from 1962 to 1963 and 1964 and the MONS Defence Officers' Cadet Training College, Aldershot, UK, January to November 1963. The Centre equally reported that he was also at the School of Infantry, Warminster, United Kingdom, in 1966 and 1971, and was at Command and Staff College, Jaji, 1976. He also attended the National Institute for Policy and Strategic studies, Kuru, Jos, Plateau State in 1981. The report had it that he was commissioned into the army as a second lieutenant in 1963 and by 1984 was a Major-General. It also stated that he was appointed Army Chief of Staff and member of the Armed Forces Ruling Council (AFRC) in 1985. Thereafter, he was appointed the Defence Secretary during the Interim National Government headed by Chief Ernest Shonekan after President Babangida's exit from power in 1993. The Biography Centre (1999) also stated that Abacha took over the reign of government on November17, 1993, from Shonekan.

General Abacha's administration demonstrated real military dictatorship, going by the records of events during his regime. Burns (1978) had earlier argued that the essential strategy of leadership is mobilizing power to articulate and realize the motives and goals of followers but this did not prove to be the case during Abacha's regime. Rather than use power as a tool to transform the society (Eghagha, 2003) he appropriated power as a vehicle for self- aggrandizement and oppression. He did not leave anyone in doubt that he was in charge. According to Justice Aguda (1998), between January 1, 1994 and June 7, 1998, Nigeria and Nigerians suffered the tyranny and brutality of Military Administration such as they had never suffered before. He further stated that the tyranny and brutality became fiercer and fiercer every day until it attained its zenith in June 1998. During this period Abacha got the former Head of State and Commander in Chief of the Armed Forces, General Obasanjo, and his former deputy, General Yar'Adua, charged and convicted for a failed coup. They would have been executed the military style, but for the intervention and outcry of the international communities. Their punishments were later converted to long-term imprisonment. General Obasanjo survived and was released out of the prison by General Abdusalami Abubakar in 1998, but his former deputy was not so lucky, because he died earlier while serving the prison sentence. Chief M.K.O. Abiola was also kept in prison against the order of a supreme court judge. He later died in custody before he could be released, just after the death of Abacha. General Diya, Abacha's deputy also narrowly escaped death by firing squad under Abacha's regime, for his involvement in a failed coup as reported by Abacha's government. He was later given long-term imprisonment instead of death by firing squad. General Diya was also later released from the prison in 1998, and is lucky to be alive today.

Apart from Abacha's high-powered dictatorship, there were serious cases of stolen funds stacked away in various foreign banks being pursued against him and members of his family for recovery by the Federal Government (2003). The Punch Editorial (Nov. 14, 2003) reported that the Federal Government was putting finishing touches to the recovery of the $618 million Abacha loot trapped in Switzerland. The Swiss Government started the legal process for the repatriation almost immediately and part of the funds had already been repatriated as reported by the Federal Ministry of Finance (2004). London

Times Report (Cited in Scrutiny, July 1998) stated that General Abacha had 3.6 billion pounds Sterling salted away in foreign accounts. He died unexpectedly while still in office in June 1998. It could again here be said that General Abacha's regime could not promote effective leadership in Nigeria. The legacy he left was not positive to support development of effective and exemplary leadership in Nigeria as is the focus of this research, because of the corruption and oppression associated with his leadership. His political leadership was a failure that brought terrible hardship.

◆ ◆ ◆

The Eleventh Head Of State, 1998 – Gen. Abdusalami Abubakar (RTD)

General Abubakar was born on the 13th of June 1942, in Minna, Niger State, and he married Justice Fatima and they have two sons and three daughters (Nigerian International Biography Centre, 1999). He had his primary education at Native Authority Primary School, Minna, from 1950 to 1956. The Centre also reported that he went to the Provincial Secondary School, Bida, from 1957 to 1962, and to the Technical Institute, Kaduna, 1963. The report also had it that he was at the Nigerian Defence Academy, Kaduna, from 1963 to 1966, and attended Infantry Officers' Course in the U.S.A., from 1975 to 1976, and the Airborne Course, USA, in 1976. It was also stated that he attended the Command and Staff College, Jaji, 1977, and the Senior Officers' Defence Management Course, in 1982. He attended the Senior Executive Course at National Institute for Policy and Strategic Studies, Kuru, Jos, in 1985.

According to the Biography Centre (1999) he started his military career with the Infantry Corps, Nigerian Army, 1967 and he became Battalion Second-in-Command, and General Officer 2, 2 Division Garrison, from 1967 to 1968. He became the Commanding Officer, from 1969 to 1974, and Brigade Major, 7 Infantry Brigade, from 1974 to 1975. It was also reported that he was with the Nigerian Army Military Service, United Nations Peace-Keeping Force, Lebanon, from 1978 to 1979, and became the Commanding Officer, 84 Infantry Battalion; Assistant Adjutant-General, 3 Infantry Division; Commanding Officer, 145 Infantry Battalion, from 1978 to 1979. He was the Chief Instructor, Nigerian Defence Academy, from 1980 to 1982. From 1982 to 1984, according to the report, he was the Colonel, Administration and Quartering, 1 Mechanised Division. He became Commander, 3 Mechanised Brigade from 1984 to 1985. He was promoted Colonel in 1985 and became Commander, 9 Mechanised Brigade, from 1985 to 1986. The report stated that he became the Military Secretary, Nigerian Army, from 1986 to 1988. He was Member, Armed Forces Ruling Council, and General Officer Commanding, 82 Division, Enugu, from 1988 to 1990. He became the Commandant, Nigeria Army School of Infantry, 1990, and General Officer Commanding, 1 Mechanised Division, Kaduna, from 1990 to 1991. The Biography Centre (1999) also reported that he became Chief of Policy and Plans, Nigerian Army, from 1991 to 1993, and Chief of Defence Staff, from 1995 to 1998, and that he was promoted a General in 1998.

After the death of General Abacha in office he became the Head of State and Commander-in-Chief of the Armed Forces from 1998 to 1999 when he retired after conducting the election and handing over to General Obasanjo who was democratically elected in 1999 (Government Press Release, 1999). General Abdusalami Abubakar, as the most senior army officer still in service, and as the Chief of Defence Staff then, took over the leadership of the country after the death of General Abacha. He had to face the enormous task of handling the politically volatile country that Abacha left behind. He seemed to understand the state of the nation then, and mobilized power to articulate and realize the motives and goals of the followers (Burns, 1978). According to Government Press Release (1998) he went on to arrest and to detain some of the Abacha's military strongmen like Major Hamza and his group who were out to derail the government. He released those who were kept behind bars by Abacha for their involvement in military coups. He released General Obasanjo and Diya from their various prisons. However, Chief M.K.O. Abiola, died in government custody during his time, (Government Press Release, 1998) and this was a major dent for his administration, but he managed it well.

He worked very hard to conduct democratic election to hand power back to democratically elected political leader. He conducted the election in 1998 and General Obasanjo, a former military head of state and the former prisoner emerged the winner. General Abdulsalami and his colleagues in the military, drafted the 1999 constitution and formally handed power over to General Obasanjo after swearing him in as a democratically elected head of state in May 1999, just after about ten months of coming to power in 1998. His leadership will always be remembered for handing over peacefully to democratically elected leader and for saving Nigeria from total collapse.

The Twelfth Head of State, 1999 –
Gen. Olusegun Obasanjo (RTD)

The Independent National Electoral Commission (INEC) (1999) declared Chief Olusegun Obasanjo as the winner of the 1999 election, and he was therefore sworn in as the 12th Nigerian Head of State on the 29th of May 1999, according to the Nigerian Constitution. As has been stated before, he once was a military head of state after the assassination of General Murtala Muhammed, from 1976 to 1979. This was indeed his second time in office as the Nigerian head of state. The difference here is that he was democratically elected in 1999 as against the undemocratic military appointment in 1976. It was therefore expected that he had some past experience to draw from as a former head of state.

He made a heart-warming speech (Obasanjo, 1999), at the swearing-in ceremony in Abuja, particularly on how corruption would be wiped out and effective leadership offered to Nigerians. The presidential inaugural speech as reproduced below needs serious review because the speech is loaded with facts about the performance of past leadership. The inaugural speech was like an official indictment and confirmation that most of the past Nigerian leaders, both military and civilians, but the military leaders in particular were corrupt and therefore responsible for the poor performance of the economy and the very slow rate of development and growth in the country. It will therefore be useful to review this, in the light of Chief Olusegun Obasanjo's performance so far. This will help to establish whether he has been able to make any difference and positive impact on the leadership of the country.

The Chief Olusegun Obasanjo's Inaugural Speech on 29th May 1999.

"Corruption, the greatest single bane of our society today, will be tackled head-on at all levels. Corruption is incipient in all human societies and in most human activities. But it must not be condoned. This is why laws are made and enforced to check corruption, so that society would survive and develop in an orderly, reasonable and predictable way. No society can achieve anything near its full potential if it allows corruption to become the full-blown cancer it has become in Nigeria. One of the greatest tragedies of military rule in recent times is that corruption was allowed to grow unchallenged, and unchecked, even when it was glaring for everybody to see. The

rules and regulations for doing official business were deliberately ignored, set aside or bye-passed to facilitate corrupt practices. The beneficiaries of corruption in all forms will fight back with all the foul means at their disposal. We shall be firm with them. There will be no sacred cows. Nobody, no matter who and where, will be allowed to get away with the breach of the law or the perpetration of corruption and evil.

Under this administration, therefore, all the rules and regulations designed to help honesty and transparency in dealings with government will be restored and enforced. Specifically, I shall immediately reintroduce "Civil Service Rules" and "Financial Instructions" and enforce compliance. Other regulations will be introduced to ensure transparency. The rampant corruption in the public service and the cynical contempt for integrity that pervades every level of the bureaucracy will be stamped out. The public officer must be encouraged to believe once again that integrity pays. His self-respect must be restored and his work must be fairly rewarded through better pay and benefits, both while in service and in retirement."

Unfortunately, more than five years after, despite the promise that the rampant corruption in the public services and the cynical contempt for integrity that pervades every level of the bureaucracy will be stamped out, Justice Mustapha Akanbi (2004) still recognized corruption as a very serious setback for any meaningful development in Nigeria. The well- respected Judge came up with this view after heading the Independent Corrupt Practices and other related offences Commission (ICPC) for over four years. He went further to say that corruption threatens Nigeria's democracy. Apart from this, the report from the United States (US) General Accounting Office (2004) warns that corruption in sub-Saharan Africa is still wide-spread and severally undercuts the region's long-term economic growth and development, often diverting funds that could be used for education, investment and public infrastructure. The report details U.S. anti-corruption projects that are part of its assistance programmes to sub-Saharan Africa but cautions that, even though corruption in the region is widespread, measuring it is "inherently challenging". The report went further to state that the World Bank Index and Transparency International Index rank many sub-Saharan African nations including Nigeria, among the most corrupt worldwide, but says that both indices rely on perceptions rather than quantifiable incidences of corruption, and both institutions recognize that their assessments are imprecise.

In addition, the United Nations Industrial Development Organization (2004) stated in the new report released after an extensive survey of the economic and social conditions of the nations in sub-Saharan Africa Countries, that these countries are poorer today than they were 20 years ago, adding that abject poverty had grown in the countries of sub-Saharan Africa and that those living in absolute poverty in the region rose from 42% in 1981 to 47% in 2001. The report also singled out Nigeria as a nation with the worst case of capital flight in the region, with more than $100 billion private wealth kept abroad, representing an estimated 70% of the nation's total private wealth. The United Nations Industrial Development Organization (UNIDO) report stated that having such amount outside the country is an indication of insecurity at home, which would make it difficult to convince foreigners to bring in their money as a direct investment. In support of this same argument, the World Bank Chief, Prof Joseph Stiglitz (2004) stated that the stashing of funds abroad by Nigerians was direct response to the unfavourable investment climate in the country.

The UNIDO report further explained that the nation could be on the path to economic recovery if government could get these funds to be returned and invested at home first before seeking foreign investment. The explanation and advice seem to be right more so as the report urged Nigeria to borrow a leaf from Uganda, which had the same problem of huge capital flight by its citizens as at 1990. UNIDO reported that the Ugandan government worked hard throughout the nineties, to get the money back to its territory and by so doing were able in some years to get the capital repatriation flow larger than export earnings. The UNIDO report also noted that the poverty level of nations in sub-Saharan Africa would not change unless their leaders would strive to enthrone good governance and macroeconomic management. The report also suggested that the leaders must also develop the private sector, diversify their economies and dramatically improve agricultural productivity.

In view of all these it can therefore be said that the president is yet to stamp out corruption in the public services, and make the economy grow, and eradicate or reduce poverty in Nigeria. Burns (1978), quoted earlier, stated that the essential strategy of leadership is mobilizing power to articulate and realize the motives and goals of followers. It must however, be acknowledged that the president emphasized that the public officer must be encouraged that integrity pays. The focus of this research is on the effects of integrity as a major leadership trait on effective leadership. It is therefore interesting and encouraging to note that despite the reported level of corruption in the country, integrity is still recognized as one of the major factors that could promote effective and outstanding leadership. The detailed discussions on this in chapter five below were quite convincing. However, from all the evidence around and the argument so far, the promise by the president to wage a total war on corruption remained unfulfilled. The President, Chief Obasanjo (1999) in his inaugural speech said: "There will be no sacred cows. Nobody, no matter who and where, will be allowed to get away with the breach of the law or the perpetration of corruption and evil".

It was very disheartening and disappointing to note that the former Inspector-General of Nigerian Police, Tafa Balogun, who was reporting directly to the President, stole and laundered about N16.3 billion (Economic and Financial Crimes Commission (EFCC), 2005), under the watchful eyes of the President within the short period he was in office. However, because of the positive impact of this discovery on the Nigerian economic environment, the credit must go to EFCC who was able to investigate and discover all the details that finally led to the successful conviction and sentencing of the former Inspector-General of Police.

As reported by the Federal High Court in Abuja (22nd of November 2005), Tafa Balogun pleaded guilty to the eight count charges and was convicted and jailed for four years and eight months. Justice Binta Murtala-Nyako who sentenced him to six months imprisonment on each of the eight counts said they were to run concurrently. In effect, he spent only six months in jail. The court also ordered the former Inspector-General to pay a fine of four million Naira. The eight companies charged with him also pleaded guilty and were ordered to forfeit all their assets to the Federal Government and to wind up immediately. The Corporate Affairs Commission (CAC) was also instructed to strike off their names from the list of registered companies in the country. This case had shown the world that there was indeed corruption in high places in Nigeria and strongly supported our argument in this research that leadership with integrity can offer a good solution to Nigerian leadership problem and poor economic growth, rather than the economic packages often prescribed by the IMF and World Bank. Part of the argument of this study is that Nigeria needs leaders with integrity who will be trustworthy (Kouzes and Posner, 2002), transparent, committed and able to render services to the nation effectively like leaders in the developed countries, rather than the leadership that have opted to appropriate power as a vehicle for self- aggrandisement and oppression (Eghagha, 2003). The lesson from the former Inspector General's case had proved that the war against corruption should be total and should not have any sacred cow. Obasanjo had been accused by the political opponents for being selective in the fight against corruption and he was yet to prove his opponents wrong and win the total support from the citizens for this noble fight by walking his talk.

A good and practical example of this seeming double standard was the protracted leadership and political disputes in Anambra State in which a political godfather, Chris Uba, openly and consistently wanted the Governor of the state to resign from office so that he could replace him with the deputy who would probably obey all his command. The political godfather claimed that he was the one that put the Governor in office. By interpretation this meant that the voting of the people did not matter in selecting the governor. On one occasion, the political godfather organized the abduction of the Governor of the state with the Assistant Inspector General of police in attendance. This was announced over the Anambra State radio, but the abduction was not so successful. The deputy governor lost out, and the top police officer who said that he acted on the orders from above was also retired by the Federal Government. He died soon after in his village in Kogi State. The dispute in Anambra State continued to escalate and was taking national dimension with loss of lives and properties and Nigerians started complaining openly in the various news media. At this point the President through press interview (2004) opened up, to tell the nation that the dispute had a moral issue because the Governor and his political godfather were like two armed robbers who were quarrelling over the sharing of their loots after a robbery. Obasanjo, the President told the nation that Chris Uba, the godfather had once in the President's house and presence told the Governor (Chris Ngige) that he did not win the election and that he knew what he did to put the governor there. According to the President, the Governor did not challenge the statement as false. This was like an open confession for a serious act of election rigging that should have attracted immediate arrest and punishment if the war against corruption were to be total. It could therefore be said that the President did not fight this serious act of corruption and this failure seemed to support the argument of the opposition and the critics that he had been selective in his fight against corruption. Chris Uba, the political godfather, despite all these revelations was still not arrested for prosecution for such a serious offence. He was only briefly expelled from the political party (PDP) together with the Governor Chris Ngige. He was however, later recalled back to the party and was given a bigger appointment within the party as a member of the board of trustee representing the Southeast. The governor who was expelled at the same time with him was left out in the cold to face the election tribunal judgment that eventually declared his election null and void in 2005, after a very long delay and legal battle.

Alhaji Musa Yar'Adua was born into a Fulani Aristocratic family in Katsina State on August 16, 1951. His father was a former Minister for Lagos during the First Republic. He attended Rafukka Primary School in 1958, and in 1962 he changed to Dutsinma Boarding Primary School. He had his secondary education at Government College Keffi from 1965 to 1969. He attended Ahmadu Bello University, Zaria, between 1972 and 1975 and obtained B.Sc., in Education and Chemistry. In 1978, he obtained his M.Sc, in Analytical Chemistry from the same University. Yar'Adua worked as a teacher at Holy Child College in Lagos, between 1975 and 1976. He became a lecturer at the College of Arts, Science and Technology, Zaria between 1976 and 1979. He later joined corporate world at Sambo Farms Ltd in Funtua, Katsina State, as the pioneer general manager between 1983 and 1989. He served as a Board member of Katsina State Farmers Supply Company between 1984 and 1985. He was a member of the Governing Council of Katsina College of Arts, Science and Technology Zaria and Katsina Polytechnic between 1978 and 1983. He was the board chairman of Katsina State Investment and Property Development Company between 1994 and 1996. He also served as director of many companies including Habib Nigeria Bank Ltd, 1995 to 1999, Lodigiani Nigeria Ltd, from 1987 to 1999, Hamada Holdings, from 1983 to 1999, and Madara Ltd, Von, Jos, from 1987 to 1999. He was also the chairman of Nation House Press Ltd, Kaduna, from 1995 to 1999.

Umaru Yar'Adua married Turai Umaru Yar.Adua of Katsina in 1975, they had seven children, five daughters and two boys. Their daughter Zainab is married to Kebbi State governor, Usman Saidu Nasamu Dakingari. The other daughter, Nafisat is married to Bauchi State governor, Isa Yuguda. He also married a second wife named Hauwa Umar Radda from 1992 to 1997. The marriage was blessed with two children.

In the year 1999, Umaru Musa Yar'Adua contested for the governorship of Katsina State and won. He therefore worked as the executive governor of Katsina State from 1999 to 2003. He was re-elected in the year 2003 for second term and he went on to complete the second term as the executive governor of Katsina State in 2007.

In 2007, under the leadership of President Obasanjo, he won the PDP primary to contest as the presidential candidate of the party. In April 2007, he contested for the position of the president of the Federal Republic of Nigeria and won. He became the President and was sworn in in May 2007. After the election, he proposed a government of national unity. In late June 2007 two opposition parties, the ANPP and Progressive Peoples Alliance (PPA) agreed to join his government. On 28 June he publicly revealed his declaration of assets from May, and this made him the first Nigerian leader to do so. He worked as the President of Nigeria and made some remarkable decisions like the amnesty for the Niger Delta fighters. Relative peace and economic activities returned to Niger Delta and oil exploration and exportation went on the increase as a result.

On November 23, 2009, Umaru Musa became very ill and was flown overseas to Saudi Arabia. He was reported to be receiving treatment for pericarditis. The treatment was prolonged and he was not able to carry on with his political leadership responsibilities for a long period. This created a dangerous power vacuum in Nigeria. On 22 January 2010, the Supreme Court of Nigeria ruled that the Federal Executive Council (FEC) had fourteen days to decide a resolution on whether Yar'Adua was incapable of discharging the functions of his office. The ruling also stated that the Federal Executive Council should hear the testimony of five doctors, and that one of them should be Yar'Adua's personal physician. Tension was on the increase and mistrust grew in the land due to the secrecy surrounding the health of the Nigerian president.

On the 10 February 2010, the Senate used the doctrine of necessity to transfer presidential powers to the Vice President Goodluck Jonathan, and declared him Acting President, with all the powers until Yar'Adua returned to full health. On the 24th February 2010, Yar'Adua returned to Abuja under the cover of darkness. His state of health was not clear and there was speculation that he was still on life support machine. He died on the 5th of May 2010 at Aso Rock Presidential Villa. His burial took place on the 6th of May 2010 in his home town in Katsina. It is indeed difficult to accurately assess the leadership performance of President Musa Yar'Adua because his health challenge was a serious obstacle. He exhibited good courage and moral example by being the first President that declared his assets publicly. He did not stay healthy and long enough in office to prove himself and this created a power vacuum. The cabals in his government took advantage and exploited the situation and created problems of instability that was eventually solved by the senate using the doctrine of necessity.

The Fourteenth Head Of State, 2010
– Dr Goodluck Ebele Jonathan

Jonathan was born in Otuoke, Ogbia Local Government, Bayelsa State, to the family of Lawrence Ebele Jonathan, a family of canoe makers on the 20th of November 1957. His mother, Mrs Eunice Ayi Ebele Jonathan is a retired farmer. He was brought up in his village and he reported that he went to school without shoes because his parents could not afford one for him. His early childhood hardship did not stop him from struggling to get good education. He was educated at St Stephen's Primary School Otuoke, St Michael's Primary School Oloibiri, Mater Dei High School, Imiringi Ogbia. He was able to pursue his education to University level. He holds a Second-Class Honours degree (BSc degree in Zoology) from the University of Port Harcourt. He also holds an MSc degree in Hydrobiology and Fisheries biology, and PhD degree in Zoology and all from the same university. He started his political career with the return of democracy in Nigeria in 1998. Diepreye Alamieyeseigha, the governorship candidate for PDP chose Dr Goodluck Ebele Jonathan to be his running mate. They won the election and Goodluck Jonathan became the first civilian Deputy Governor of Bayelsa State on May 29 1999. They were re-elected in 2004. Before then he worked as an education inspector, lecturer, and environmental protection officer. He got married to Patience Faka Jonathan and they have two children. Jonathan is a Christian and from the Ijaw ethnic group.

He remained the deputy governor of Bayelsa until the governor was impeached by the Bayelsa State Assembly after being charged with money laundering in the United Kingdom in 2005. On the 9th December 2005, Jonathan was sworn in as Governor of Bayelsa State following the impeachment of his boss. He did not plan this nor asked for it, but luck brought this to him. There is something in a name they said. He carried on as the Governor of the state. Towards the end of this term in 2007, another luck came his way again without him asking for it. President Obasanjo was planning for his successors in office. He succeeded in getting Alhaji Musa Yar'Adua as the presidential candidate for the PDP and Dr Goodluck Jonathan as his running mate. The candidates from the People Democratic Party won the election in April 2007 general election. Musa Yar'Adua and Dr Goodluck Jonathan were sworn in on 29th May 2007 as President and Vice President respectively. Dr Goodluck Jonathan's luck did not end here as events continued to unfold in his favour. In all these unfolding events one could be tempted to state that God's hands were on Jonathan to make him a leader for Nigeria without him struggling for it. Much was given to him. To whom much is given, much is expected. The big question is: did Dr Goodluck Jonathan deliver good leadership for Nigeria in view of the golden opportunity given to him?

As Vice President he took a low profile recognising the constitutional limitation of the Vice President. He participated in cabinet meetings, National Defence Council, and Federal Executive Council. He was the chairman of the National Economic Council. He played an important role in the negotiation agreement with many of the major militant group in Niger Delta who were mostly of Ijaw ethnic group like himself. They eventually laid down their arms as part of the amnesty agreement. He served as Vice President of Nigeria from 2007 to 2010 and was sworn in as President of the Federal Republic of Nigeria on the 6th of May 2010, following the death of President Umaru Musa Yar'Adua on the 5th of May 2010. He therefore became the 14th Nigerian Head of State. He cited anti-corruption, power, and electoral reforms as focuses of his administration. He stated that he came to office under very sad and unusual circumstances. He nominated the former Kaduna State governor, Namadi Sambo for the position of Vice President and the National Assembly approved this on the 18th of May 2010. He continued with the seven-point agenda policy framework of President Musa Yar'Adua.

On the 15th September 2010 Jonathan announced his decision to run for public office on his own for the first time for the presidency of Nigeria in 2011. He contested for the PDP nomination against the former Vice President, Atiku Abubakar and Mrs Sarah Jubril and won. For the general election in 2011 he contested against General Muhammadu Buhari and his running mate Pastor Tunde Bakare and won and on the 18th of April he was declared the winner of the election. He therefore remained the President of the Republic of Nigeria from 2011 to 2015 when he contested the 2015 general election. Some credit must be given to him for some electoral reforms and promotion of democracy. He made a good choice by appointing Professor Jega as the Chairman of INEC. He did a good job in the power sector with the help of the power minister, Professor Chinedu Osita Nebo. He demonstrated high moral value by recognising that no Nigerian blood is worth shedding for political power. This can partly explain why he conceded defeat and rejected the advice of those who wanted him to fight on and get electoral victory at all costs. Goodluck Jonathan will also be remembered as a Nigerian leader that stood against the interest and pressure of the western world leaders and the U.S. He damned the consequences and went ahead to sign into law, the anti-gay marriage and homosexual bill by the National Assembly. There is no doubt that these world leaders made sure he paid dearly for standing up against their immoral and unholy standard. He lost political power but Nigerians and indeed Africans will always remember that he did not let them down morally and religiously.

However, Jonathan lacked the political will to deal decisively with corruption. He could have achieved better results for Nigeria if he had stayed with the one term political agreement rather than wasting his time negotiating and trying to please the stakeholders to have a second term. He lost the strong fol- lowership of his party as a result and above all he did not get the second term. The influence of power must have overwhelmed him, and he lost the chance to be the great leader that Niger- ians have been looking for. This becomes more disappointing when we remember how he came to power on a platter of gold. He got to position of leadership without much struggles where some great Nigerian politicians could not get to irrespective of their skills, experience and wealth. He was indeed lucky, and this is a confirmation that there is something in a name. He con- tested and lost 2015 presidential election. He became the first Nigerian president to concede defeat and his term as Nigerian president ended on the 29th of May 2015. Muhammadu Buhari became the new president.

The Fifteenth Head Of State, 2015 –
Gen Muhammadu Buhari (RTD)

General Buhari (rtd) as stated earlier was the 7th head of state of Nigeria in 1983 when he came to power through military coup that toppled Alhaji Shehu Shagari. He was overthrown by General Babangida in a counter coup that took place in 1985 and was subsequently imprisoned. He regained his freedom but was retired from the military service. He later started making attempts to gain power to rule Nigeria through democratic means. His first attempt was in 1999 when he was defeated by Obasanjo. He protested and went through election tribunal and all the way to supreme court but lost. It was not easy for him to gain power democratically but he kept trying. He tried in 2003, 2007, and 2011 subsequently, but failed all the way after fighting it out through the court of law. However, luck smiled at him in 2015 when he defeated the incumbent president, Dr Goodluck Ebele Jonathan. It must be stated clearly that it took the help and teaming together with Bola Tinubu of Lagos State, and other political parties to form a mega party APC, for this victory to be realised. Tinubu virtually was responsible for the western Nigerian votes that made the victory possible. He mobilised support for him and ensured that Buhari won the primary of the APC. Nigerians were desperate for a change and when Buhari promised to fight corruption and redeem the image of the country many Nigerians believed him and voted for change. They saw him as a man of integrity that will deliver Nigeria. It is however, sad that the taste of the pudding is in the eating.

The first sign that all is not well was that it took six months for the president to assemble members of his cabinet who were expected to be experts that will help the president to deliver the change. The newly elected president was sensitive at that point to note that Nigerians were getting impatient, because he jokingly stated that people were already referring to him as "baba go-slow". The government was eventually formed and all the necessary appointments made and actions started. Almost immediately, things started moving rather slowly indeed. Before then the national leader was seen to be all over the place and influencing lots of actions and who gets what. The struggle for leadership of the national assembly came up and went the other way. It appeared some cabals were taking over control quietly. Before long the first lady complained publicly during an interview with BBC, against those that were reaping where they did not sow. This was compounded when the president went public to talk about his wifes place in the 'other room'. All these appeared revealing and entertaining but quite significant politically. Nigerians remained shock absorbers, hopeful and resilient and could tolerate what most people of the world would not accept. The expectation for effective leadership and serious fight against corruption continued and Nigerians remained hopeful.

However, the complaints against the cabal continued beyond the first lady and other political leaders from the north have joined the criticism. The Federal character principles were not strictly followed and those that were given the jobs have no proof that they got them on merit as such. Economic activities and governance were rather slow generally. The economy was getting worse and the unemployment rate kept moving higher. The system started heating up and the general outcry continued from the public and even the national assembly added their voice to demand for reshuffling and sacking of the members of the cabinet to ensure better results. The President as a leader could not promptly react to these challenges. Before coming to power, he had been perceived as a man of integrity who could fix all Nigerian problems within a short period. It was therefore disturbing and disappointing to observe these early signs of leadership failures.

The first serious dent on the war against corruption by Buhari government came when a publication appeared, alleging that the Chief of Staff of the Army purchased two buildings worth seventy- five million dollars, in Dubai. This was treated as fake news, but later confirmed as real and that the properties were legitimately purchased with savings. There was no investigation publicly, to prove that a public officer could save such amount within a limited period. Nigerians continued to move on with expectation for dividends of democracy to be delivered by the President.

The ill -health and absence of the President from the seat of power did not help matters. The cabals were seen to have taken over for real and prevented the public from knowing the true health situation of their president.   Within two years of this leadership, top members of this government had been accused of high level of corruption but were not removed from office. The law did not take its course. It took continuous pressure from the national assembly and outcry from the press for the Secretary to the Federal Government (SGF) and the Director-General of the National Intelligence Agency to be suspended from their various offices. It was reported that the SGF,   awarded grass cutting contract for the IDP camp, for about two hundred million Naira to his private company. It was discovered that the DG of NIA, stacked billions of Naira and millions of dollars and pounds sterling in a private building in Ikoyi, Lagos State.

These top level officers were eventually suspended from office and proper investigation conducted by the Vice President and the committee appointed by the government.

In another disturbing case, the senate refused to confirm the acting chairman of EFCC based on the indicting report presented against him by the Department of State Security (DSS), but the President insisted on retaining him for the job Except if there is any hidden agenda, a report from government agency like DSS, should be seen to be serious but the President insisted that it must be Magu and nobody else. This was another disturbing signal. Nigeria is filled with many talented people that the President could have picked from. For the fight against corruption to succeed it must be total and not limited. The fight against corruption by EFCC has not been seen by the public to be convincingly total and fair on all

Lack of serious and decisive actions seem to be encouraging more and more scandals within the government. Nigerians were still listening and digesting the accusation for corruption, and the legal argument between the Inspector General of Police (IGP) and a current Senator, Isa Misau. They were wondering why the IGP should prefer to go to court, instead of allowing the senate to investigate the case of corruption brought against him by Senator Isa Misau. As if that was not enough worry other scandals were taking the front stage. Maina reinstatement came to the public knowledge and was another serious scandal with complex dimension involving Mr Maina, the AGF and the Minister of Justice as well as the Minister of Interior. It came to the public knowledge that Mr Maina, a former chairman of task force for pension fraud prevention, committed fraud of one hundred billion Naira. He had been on the wanted list of the EFCC since 2013. He was also dismissed by the civil service commission in 2015. Despite all these recorded offences, he was recalled by the Attorney General of the Federation. He directed the Federal Civil Service Commission to reabsorb Maina and post him to the Ministry of Interior on promotion with the approval of the Minister of Interior. This was indeed a heavy blow on the integrity of Mr President.

This appears to be the mother of all scandals and a serious action against the public interest. There was serious public outcry against this action that lacks integrity. The press reported that the President issued a public statement sacking Mr Maina from the Ministry of Interior. However, the AGF and the Minister of Interior were not given the boot despite the effects on the public trust. There is no doubt that this is another serious dent on the integrity of the leadership. To make the matter worse, the Maina family had the audacity to accuse the government of wrong doing by sacking their son after calling him home to come and help in the change agenda. All these are serious dent and distraction to the goals set by President Buhari. It appears that these corrupt subordinates have no integrity or that they do not believe in the fight against corruption.

It is therefore very important that these distractors should be shown the way out to ensure that this leadership will make meaningful headway and sustain the confidence. There is strong need to bark and bite to convince Nigerians. The president has the power and responsibility to discipline all the subordinates whenever they default, to convince the followers that he leads by example. Buhari's leadership needs more action here because this is the 21st century when the followers are getting better informed and therefore can read between the lines. There is need for him to try and win the confidence and trust of the people. Nigerians as a people are easily pleased and not as demanding as their counterparts in other parts of the world and this may partly explain why Nigerian politicians are exploiting their citizens by not giving good account of their stewardship.

The President being the commander in chief of the Federation has the power and resources to provide security for all Nigerians. He has the power to deal with any insurgence as he has demonstrated in the past. The issue of the armed Fulani herdsmen, who have been terrorising and killing farmers in different parts of the country, like Benue, Ekiti, Ondo, Ebonyi, Enugu, Osun, Jos, Adamawa and other places is another serious dent on the leadership. The agriculture policy of this administration will not succeed if the farmers are continuously chased away from their farms by the armed herdsmen who are only interested in feeding their cows and destroying the farmers crops. The President should rise to this challenge and bring these killers to book and win the trust of Nigerians. Integrity in leadership is all about being transparently honest in all the decisions and actions of the leader. Nigeria is a big country with big potentials to accommodate all the citizens. Any leader that has the strong moral will to apply integrity and fairness to all the citizens will achieve outstanding results and will be celebrated as a hero.

President Buhari has completed his first term of four years but nothing has changed, if anything the insecurity of lives and properties have been on the serious increase and lack of trust within the country has gone beyond control. He started his second term in May, 2019, having won the presidential election that was marred with violence and serious electoral malpractices. The PDP presidential candidate, Alhaji Atiku Abubakar felt he won the election and therefore challenged the results from tribunal court all the way to the supreme court where he also lost.

He made some changes in his new cabinet but his leadership style has not changed. The insecurity of lives and properties have continued to be the worry of the people of Nigeria. The northern elders and youths are now champions in challenging his inability to provide adequate security for the country. They have called on him to sack his service chiefs and replace them with new ones because the old seemed to have run out of ideas. The Boko Haram has been terrorising the northern parts of the country. The Fulani herdsmen and kidnappers are terrorising people all over the country and fuelling the agitation for restructuring the country. The economy is not doing well and unemployment has continued to rise. As a matter of fact, the President has been called upon to resign by the northern elders and other concerned citizen. The nation is going through a difficult time of disunity and mistrust due to the President's style of leadership. His appointments are lopsided and favours mainly the northern parts of the country and particular religion, without serious consideration of the Federal character. He got the votes that gave him victory from all parts of the country and so the entire country is expected to be his constituency. It could therefore be said that he has not delivered what he promised the country and that integrity as a pillar that holds and promotes outstanding leaders has not been given its rightful place.

◆ ◆ ◆

The Summary Of The Reviews And The Impact Of Past Political Leadership In Nigeria

From the above reviews and analysis, it could be said that Nigeria has been a country blessed with abundant natural resources with great potentials for growth and greatness (National Planning Commission, 2004). The resources are still in abundance, waiting to be effectively tapped and converted for economic growth through effective management and leadership. Most Nigerians will agree that Nigeria has what it takes to be a great nation going by her abundant resources. However, as revealed above the country had been saddled with the problem of ineffective political leadership throughout the years of her existence, and the verdict is that most leaders, military or civilian have failed the Nigerian people (Eghagha, 2003). Obasanjo (1999) said: "One of the greatest tragedies of military rule in recent times is that corruption was allowed to grow unchallenged, and unchecked, even when it was glaring for everybody to see. The rules and regulations for doing official business were deliberately ignored, set aside or bye-passed to facilitate corrupt practices." From this review it is quite clear that Obasanjo had chance to rule Nigeria twice, first as a military dictator in 1976 and later in 1999 as a democratic leader, but in all he could not deliver Nigeria from corruption even when he had the opportunity to do so. In summary, Nigeria produced fifteen Heads of State just between 1960 and 2019 and some of these lasted only for few months. One thing that appeared very common and consistent throughout the history of this country is the lack of trust (Kouzes and Posner, 2002) between the leaders and the led and between the various ethnic groups as shown in the various accounts above. All these failed political leadership have impacted negatively on the Nigerian organizations and the leadership at various levels. Corruption is the name of the game especially in public sector organisations despite the highly publicised fight against it. The board members of these organisations are appointed as political compensations mostly and not on merit. This can explain why these board members are more of liabilities than assets to the organisations they are sent to. The higher institutions are worse off because most of the council members appointed by the government see their appointments as opportunities to make money from the inadequate resources of such institutions. Unnecessary frequent meetings are called not for the good of such institutions but as avenue for increased allowances and depletion of the limited resources allocated to the institutions. The negative impact has spread widely like cancer and serious surgery need to be done to rescue Nigeria from the negative effects of failed leadership and poor governance.

Positive contribution to organizational leadership may not be easy without effective transformation of the conflicts that had infected the nation for too long. "Conflict transformation", is a recent but welcome addition to peace concepts (Albert, 2003). Its main goal according to Albert is to change unjust social relationships. The concept of conflict transformation is an integrative approach to conflict resolution that focuses on how human perceptions, communication and structural problems producing a conflict situation can be positively altered. It is a long-term development agenda specifically targeting all or most of the following: causing a change in the entire context of the conflict; causing a change in the conflict parties' relationship; or causing a change (e.g. through empowerment) in the individuals involved in the conflict (Burgess and Burgess, 1977: 285-286).

There is no doubt that there is need to transform the leadership conflicts that had delayed the effective development in Nigeria in order to achieve a lasting solution to the problems of leadership that could easily be noticed at all tiers of government in the country, from the national level to state level and down to local government level.

Apart from the need for conflict transformation the trait approach to leadership (Northouse, 2001) should be given the proper consideration in Nigeria. The rampant failure of leadership in Nigeria is a strong indicator for change in approach and standard expected of any person aspiring to be a leader in Nigeria. At state level, almost all the governors of the thirty- six states of the federation had so far been accused openly for corrupt practices by Economic and Financial Crime Commission (EFCC) (2005)

Two out of these governors had carried their unpatriotic and corrupt activities beyond the shores of the country to London where their so-called immunity could no longer cover their economic offences when they were caught in the net of the London Metropolitan Police for money laundering (EFCC, 2005).

They were caught red-handed with huge sums of money in their possession. The Plateau State governor, Chief Joshua Dariye, who was the first to fall into this trap succeeded in jumping bail when he was caught a year earlier. He got back to Nigeria and refused to go back to Britain to face the trial. He had taken shelter under the immunity clause 308 of Nigerian Constitution that has continued to provide shelter for corrupt governors. Chief Diepreye Alamieyeseigha, the Bayelsa State governor was not so lucky when he was arrested by the London Metropolitan Police for alleged money laundering offences of about 1.8 million pounds (EFCC, 2005). The London Police seemed to have become wiser from the earlier experience with the governor of the Plateau State. The Bayelsa State governor was therefore refused bail and was remanded in the prison custody despite the claim of immunity. However, according to the report, this treatment was relaxed later and he was placed under house arrest with some restrictions of movement to certain areas. It was amazing that the governor took advantage of this relaxed treatment and jumped bail like the Plateau State Governor in a disguised form and returned to Yenagoa, Bayelsa State (Federal Government Press Release, 2005). Many other governors were also involved one way or the other. Some managed to get away through plea bargaining.

A former Governor like James Ibori of Delta State was so smart and powerful that he could not be arrested by EFCC in Nigeria in April 2010 when his case file was reopened after the takeover by President Goodluck Jonathan. A new allegation that he embezzled N40 billion was pressed against him. He has followers big and small that could not see anything wrong with corruption maybe because they personally benefitted from corruption. He was seriously protected by these people when he was to be arrested by the EFCC. However, he fled Nigeria and EFCC requested the assistance of Interpol. He ran out of luck on 13th May 2010 when he was arrested in Dubai under Interpol arrest warrant issued from United Kingdom courts and enacted by the Metropolitan Police. He was eventually extradited to the United Kingdom where he was tried for money laundering. The international dimension of his hunt started in 2007 when the Metropolitan police raided the London office of lawyer Bhadresh Gohil. On 27 February 2012, he was accused of stealing US$250 million from the Nigerian public purse. He pleaded guilty to ten counts of money laundering and conspiracy to defraud at Southwark Crown Court, London. On the 17th of April, 2012 Ibori was sentenced to thirteen years, by Southwark Crown Court for his crimes and some of his possessions confiscated. Ibori was released from prison in December 2016 after a court order. He served only 4 years out of the 13 years he was sentenced. Unfortunately, he returned to Delta State as a hero despite all the incalculable damages he had done to the economy of the state and the poverty he inflicted on his people. This could be seen as a testimony that many Nigerians do not know their rights and are beginning to accept corruption as a smart game. This is sad indeed and cause for serious worry because corruption seems to have permeated everywhere in the society. This calls for serious re-orientation of the public.

All these are manifestation of leadership without integrity (Adair, 1983) and further dent on the image of the country as a whole, and of course, a glaring confirmation that a good number of Nigerian leaders are very corrupt and could easily abuse their powers (Eghagha, 2003). It can also be said that these ineffective leaders are responsible for the lack of development and growth of the country all these years despite the huge natural resources in the country. It is noteworthy that Bayelsa State is located in the Niger Delta, and one of the poorest and least developed state in Nigeria and yet the governor who allegedly was freely elected into office for the second term could be amassing and laundering the wealth of the poor state without caring for the need of the citizens of the state. Burns (1978) suggested that leadership is a process of morality to the extent that leaders engage with followers on the basis of shared values, motives, and goals and can help followers choose among appropriate alternatives based upon the followers' true needs.

These had confirmed the argument that some Nigerian political leaders had been a drain pipe that drained Nigerian economy to overseas countries and inflicted poverty on the citizens. It also confirmed the report of the United Nations Industrial Development Organisation (2004), that singled out Nigeria as a nation with the worst case of capital flight in the sub-Saharan region, with more than $100 billion private wealth kept abroad, representing an estimated 70% of the nation's total private wealth. It could therefore be concluded that most of the Nigerian leaders could not be said to be effective leaders in the real sense of it because they could not deliver the dividends of effective leadership as postulated in trait approach to leadership (Northouse, 2001). The process of selection or appointment of political leaders in Nigeria had remained faulty and had given opportunity to people without integrity as demonstrated above. It is the expectation in best practice that proven track records should be considered in selecting a potential leader. Prospective or potential leaders' track records should therefore be used as important instrument for assessing and determining their suitability for future higher responsibility.

A former Governor of Ogun State, commented (Press Interview, 2005) after the arrest of the Bayelsa State governor, by the British police, that the governors were endangered species, and that the governors were not poor but rich people before they got into the office as governors. He added that the nature of the Nigerian politics demand that one must spend hundreds of millions of Naira to get to the position of a governor. By this explanation, it could therefore be said that leadership in Nigerian politics is a "cash and carry" leadership. This again offers a good explanation on why the governors and other political leaders may continue to use power as vehicle for self- aggrandizement (Eghagha, 2003) and work towards ensuring that there is good return on their "huge investments" by getting directly involved in money laundering. From the Ogun State governor's statement, a governorship candidate should be rich enough to afford spending hundreds of millions to be able to get into that office. It could therefore be said that the office is not meant for the not so rich candidates even if they possessed all the traits as highlighted in trait theory (Northouse, 2001). On the other hand, it also means that any crook and irresponsible character could get into political leadership in Nigeria, if he or she had hundreds of millions of Naira to spend for the office. Effective leadership involves possession of relevant leadership profiles (Northouse, 2001), and not necessarily possession of wealth. It is therefore no wonder that people like the former Governor of Bayelsa state could get into office and amass illegal wealth, and could also readily jump bail irresponsibly to return to Nigeria from Britain, without caring about the consequences and disrespect such action could attract to him and to Nigeria.

Apart from "money bags' dominating the scene, and pushing their ways with the influence of their money, the other dangerous trend that had dominated, and prevented genuine and effective process of selection of political leaders in Nigeria, is the "godfatherism" syndrome. This was exactly the genesis of the problem in Anambra State, between Governor Chris Ngige and Chris Uba, the godfather, as reported above. The political godfathers who sponsored the elections and front effectively for the governorship candidates during elections would want to remain relevant after the victory. From the above reviews and experience so far in Nigeria, the sponsored governor's victory marked the beginning of the struggles between the governor and the "godfather", for the control of the government treasury. The end results of all these is to use power for self-aggrandisement rather than using power as a tool to transform the society (Eghagha, 2003) for the benefits of the citizens.

For the military politicians, theirs could be said to be a "do or die" leadership going by the facts reported above. They wasted as many lives as possible to get into leadership position and any coup plotters that did not succeed or got overpowered in the process got wasted too. It is leadership by coercion and Russell (1962) wrote "The man who have vast mechanical power at his command is likely, if uncontrolled, to feel himself a god – not a Christian god of Love, but a pagan Thor or Vulcan". Under the military leadership the followers had no choice than to pretend to follow for the sake of their lives with the attendant syco-phancy. There was no room for opposition, and all perceived opponents were treated like enemies. Any known corrupt acts could not be challenged without the challenger endangering his or her life. This was why President Obasanjo (1999) confirmed that one of the tragedies of military rule was that corruption was allowed to grow unchallenged and unchecked even when it was glaring.

Elaigwu (1997) in his contribution on Military Governance: The Future of Democracy in Nigeria, argued that western model of democracy cannot be transferred to Nigeria and be expected to succeed. He contended that the democratic and military in-stitutions in Nigeria must be domesticated or adapted to local conditions in the light of the country's experience and prob-lems. According to him there were major lag between these in-stitutions and the values which were supposed to underwrite them. Many of the politicians according to him had neither understood the rules of the game nor had they accepted them. Many of them see politics not as a game, but a battle. The rules are not obeyed but blatantly violated thereby making politics to become a very dangerous game. He said that the Nigerian political elite has little commitment to democracy as an end, they see it only in instrumental terms. The few elite groups that clamour for democracy as an end, for one reason or the other do not go into politics. Elaigwu (1997) made a good point when he stated that the military institution had also failed. He said that since the initial adulteration of the military in 1966, it has engaged in political promiscuity. According to him it had become a predatory institution, imploding with reckless abandon into the political arena. This was why the military had been in government for twenty- five years in Nigeria. Within the period of independence there had been ten military coups and abortive coups. Of all these, only three military coups had been against civilian regimes, and these were in January 1966, December, 1983, and in November 1993.

Professor Onoge (1995) in his paper on the theories and conceptions of leadership presented during the 3rd Obafemi Awolowo Foundation Dialogue argued that political leadership is parochial rather than national; and corruptly converts national resources into its project of primitive accumulation, and manipulate the ethnic diversity to stay afloat to the detriment of national cohesion. He also stated that the leadership problem which troubles Nigerians most is the failure of political leadership, and that other failures could be traced to political leadership deficiencies.

In view of all the above, the citizens have continued to find the political leaders, civilians or military, not worthy of their trust based on their performance so far, and the verdict is that most leaders have failed the Nigerian people (Eghagha, 2003). The followers could easily follow and support a trustworthy leader who has something good and consistent to offer them. As clearly stated by Kouzes & Posner (2002), it is clear that if people anywhere are to willingly follow someone whether it be into battle or into the boardroom, the front office or the front lines, they first want to assure themselves that the person is worthy of their trust. They want to know that the person is truthful, ethical, and principled. Nigerians must be cautious in selecting the leaders they could trust.

The selection process or the process of emergence of the political leaders in Nigeria has not sufficiently taken the trait approach to leadership (Stogdill, 1974) into consideration. Based on the comments of the existing leaders and the reported process of emergence, it could therefore be said that the selection of most of the political leaders in Nigeria were not based on their possession of certain set of traits that are crucial to having effective leadership (Northouse, 2001). Some got selected because they have the money to buy their way through or were sponsored by their godfathers. This means that potential leaders with the right set of traits but without the huge sums of money or a political godfather, may not get selected, and may never have the opportunity to lead despite having the right traits. There are signs that Nigeria has potential leaders with the right traits like integrity that could make things happen, but most of these seem not ready for the type of corrupt and "cash and carry" leadership in the country. It might be difficult for such people to emerge as political leaders in the present dispensation. The system needs overhauling if Nigeria is to get the right leaders that will lead effectively and improve organizational leadership with the promotion of real growth generally.

Trust is fundamental for effective leadership and Viscount Slim defined integrity as "the quality which makes people trust you" (Adair, 1983). It may therefore not be surprising that the political leadership in Nigeria had continued to fail and had negatively influenced leadership at other levels like the organizational level. Unlike their counterparts in the developed World, the political leadership in Nigeria had not taken good advantage of the benefits of trait approach (Stogdill, 1974) to leadership. This might be one of the reasons for the backwardness and prevailing poverty in the country. The political leadership in the developed world set the pace for the leadership at the organizational level while the political leadership in Nigeria had proved to be the obstacles due to the negative influence. The political leadership is expected to set the pace and through the higher authority and responsibility provide the good governance and enabling environment that would help the organizations operating within the country to thrive. In other words, the organizational leadership is expected to take their bearings from the good and patriotic examples of the political leadership. This was the case in the developed countries like UK, U.S.A., Japan and others. They provided the good governance and enabling environment and the organizations within thrived and faced the global competitions squarely. However, the political leadership in Nigeria have failed to match the leadership ability of their counterpart in the developed world and could not provide the enabling environment in Nigeria. The failure could be traced to corruption and mismanagement of resources as clearly revealed from the reviews above. The corrupt tendencies could be said to be carried over to the organizational leadership through the mechanism for the appointment of the leaders in the organizations, especially in the government owned organizations, where political considerations take upper hand than merits during the selection process.

Ineffective leadership at these levels had resulted to poor performance and poor economic indices. The UNDP (2000) Human Development Report, stated that no matter what human development indicator used, the country is at the bottom of the ladder. On the basis of 1999 data, it ranks in terms of its GNP, 57 while on per capita GNP basis it ranks 187. On the basis of purchasing power parity (PPP$) it ranks 51 while on a per capita PPP$ basis it ranks 194. According to the report, the human development rankings are equally very low. HDI (in 2000) puts it at 151st position whilst its GDI is a little better at 124th. In spite of all these poor indicators, Nigeria ranks 6th and 7th as petroleum exporter and producer respectively and 10th as the most populous country in the world. The report clearly stated that Nigeria's HDI value at the dawn of the third millennium and the twenty-first century puts it among the lowest of the low.

All the above indices should be a cause for worry that leadership is a serious issue that can make or mare any nation, and this is one of the reasons for this work. Effective leadership depends on trust between the leaders and the led (Kouzes and Posner, 2002), and good corporate governance seeks amongst others to promote efficient, effective and sustainable corporations that contribute to the welfare of society by creating wealth, employment and solutions to emerging challenges (Commonwealth Association for Corporate Governance, 1990). Poverty level from all the reports cited above, has continued to increase in Nigeria and the unemployment level has continued to rise. Retrenchment of the existing workers made the situation worse. It could therefore be said that rather than use power as a tool to transform society, the men and women on the leadership saddle had opted to appropriate power as a vehicle for self-aggrandizement and oppression (Eghagha, 2003). The wrong usage of power has created a sharp dissonance and gap between the supposed leaders and the led, between the rich and the poor, between the north and the south, and between Christians and the muslims (Eghagha, 2003).

The implication of bad political leadership in Nigerian environment and the consequent effects on other levels of leadership has raised some issues that bothers on the fundamentals of the trait theory of leadership and therefore need some studies that may likely contribute to knowledge in the field of leadership. It is our hope that these findings will positively contribute to the solution of the leadership problems already identified. The leadership failures are strong indicators that Nigerian leadership needs a shift towards leadership with integrity, to ensure that the leaders would lead by good example and achieve the desired results. This was why Achebe (1983), said that the trouble with Nigeria is simply and squarely a failure of leadership. He said that the Nigerian problem is the unwillingness or inability of its leaders to rise to the responsibility, to the challenge of personal example which is the hallmarks of true leadership. It must be clearly stated here that integrity in leadership is the answer to these long years of failure in Nigeria. Integrity is not word that can be used for propaganda by politicians and the highly corrupt in our society. Many leaders in Nigeria talk about integrity but there is no atom of integrity in their conducts and this must change if we want to make any headway. Leaders and potential leaders can improve tremendously in their performance if they imbibe integrity. This attribute can be developed through training as stated earlier, and potential leaders without integrity can be discovered and stopped at the entry point. This preventive action will save the country or the organisation, from the hardship of ineffective leadership. The failed leadership in Nigeria has brought pains to the country via underdevelopment and growth of poverty in the land. This is the change we need, and this book is a contribution to that effect, and more hands are needed in this direction to save Nigeria from the hands of corrupt and ineffective leaders. The results of the leadership studies with focus on the effect of integrity carried out by the author at NAFDAC and NEIMETH show that integrity holds the keys to effective leadership in Nigeria. The summaries of these studies are reported in chapters five and six below.

CHAPTER FIVE

*Data Presentation, Evaluation
and Analysis on NAFDAC
Under Prof Akunyili*

This chapter is devoted to the presentation of data, evaluation, analysis and discussions of the outcome. Firstly, the five key research questions and their corresponding hypothesis are reproduced here, together with table 5.1., showing how the questions were answered with the relevant instruments. Subsequently the reports of the interviews conducted in the first of the two selected organizations, National Agency for Food and Drug Administration and Control (NAFDAC), are presented in summary form, from section 5.1., followed by the analysis and discussions of data. The report and the presentation of data, evaluation, analysis and discussions will continue for the second organization, Neimeth International Pharmaceuticals Plc in chapter six.

The Five Research Questions And The Corresponding Hypothesis

Question 1: Can the integrity of the chief executive of the organization be confirmed by the immediate subordinates in the same organization?

Hypothesis 1: The immediate subordinates of a chief executive that has integrity will notice it, feel the impact of it, and can testify to it.

Question 2: Is there any evidence that the chief executive of the successful organization under investigation has high level of integrity?

Hypothesis 2: The success of the organization and the confirmation of the immediate subordinates will show that the chief executive of the investigated successful organization has high level of integrity.

Question 3: Is there any evidence of increase in productivity and improved performance in the organization under the leadership of the current chief executive?

Hypothesis 3: The increase in productivity and the improved performance in the investigated organization is due to the leadership ability of the current chief executive.

Question 4: Is there any evidence that the increase in productivity and improved performance of the organization has something to do with the integrity of the chief executive?

Hypothesis 4: A chief executive that has integrity will positively influence increase in productivity and improved performance in an organization.

Question 5: Is the suggestion of trait theory that organizations will work better if people in managerial positions have designated leadership profiles valid and applicable in these organizations under investigation?

Hypothesis 5: Organizations in Nigeria will work better and achieve good results if people in leadership positions have integrity.

Table 5.1. Research Questions, Instruments used and the Remarks

Research Questions	How questions were answered	Remarks
Question 1	Use of Craig & Gustafson (1998) Perceived Leader Integrity scale (PLIS), and Interview data	Provided adequate answer and supported hypothesis
Question 2	Interview data, Perceived Leader Integrity Scale (PLIS), and secondary data	Provided adequate answer and supported hypothesis
Question 3	Secondary data, Interview data	Answers adequate and in support of the hypothesis
Question 4	Interview data, Secondary data, and PLIS	Positive answers supportive of the hypothesis
Question 5	Survey Questionnaire, Interview data & Secondary data	Positive answers supportive of the hypothesis

Consideration Of The Cases To Study

There was a careful thought and consideration on whether to study cases that are unique in some way or cases that are considered typical. The issue of selecting cases to represent a variety of geographic regions, and variety of size parameters were also considered. However, the need to focus on the evidence to be gathered in order to answer the research questions became more paramount. The research exercise is to prove the validity and applicability in Nigerian context, of the trait theory that organizations will work better if people in managerial positions have designated leadership profiles (Northouse, 2001). To carry out this assignment, the researcher decided to concentrate on organizations that have been considered successful and pronounced to be so in Nigeria by the relevant national and international bodies (see exhibits 1, 2, 3, 4, 5, and 6 under appendix 4 for details on national and international recognitions, approvals, and awards), for consideration and final selection. As was stated earlier, unsuccessful organizations were not considered for this study because the researcher has adopted the approach of "In Search of Excellence" (Peters and Waterman Jr., 1982). It is the views of the researcher that the chief executive of a consistently successful organization within the difficult Nigerian economic environment will likely have a lot of good ideas to offer in a research of this nature. It is not easy to find organization whose leaders will come forward to admit that they are not successful, and be ready to grant interview on failed organization. It is difficult, especially in the third world countries, to find chief executives that will easily admit failures and be ready to grant interviews on his or her failures. These points were taken into consideration before settling to concentrate the studies on only successful organizations that could easily offer reliable data for the research.

As a result of democracy in Nigeria, government organizations and private organizations are allowed to exist side by side with their varying characteristics. This made it possible for the Nigerian economic environment to be seen and identified as two main sectors, the private sector and the public sector. These two sectors differ in their mode of operations and forces that drive them for success. The public sector as has been explained earlier is mainly the government sector and is mainly governed and driven by government policies, and influenced by bureaucracy. Organizations operating under this are usually seen to be very slow in action and heavily under the influence of government machineries. They are expected to obey the policies, rules and regulations of the government, and in accordance with these rules, the officers or managers in this system do not easily take actions on their own, on time, but do follow the general order, unless directed otherwise by the higher authority. The private sector on the other hand, is dominated by private businesses, and as has been explained earlier are driven by profit motives. Profit is seen as a major guarantee for success and growth in private organizations. The organizations here are seen to be faster in decision making and do not have to wait to be directed from the above as is the case in the public sector. The leaders of the organizations in this sector are expected to give good account of their stewardship to the shareholders or the owners of the business, through good profits and growth.

In view of all these differences, the researcher, as stated earlier, observed that selecting only one organization for the case study will not be representative enough to get precise and reliable findings (Fink, 1995a, P.34) since there are two types of sectors in existence, and the outcome from such study may not be generally applicable to the two sectors. The consideration of these problems led to the multiple cases selection to ensure that each sector is at least represented by one organization. Two organizations instead of one were therefore selected for the case study. One was from the public sector and the second one was from the private sector. The research also included limited survey amongst the immediate subordinates of the selected leaders of the two organizations, to assess the level of integrity of the leaders of the two chosen organizations, using the Perceived Leader Integrity Scale (PLIS) developed by Craig and Gustafson (1998). It also involved the analysis of some surveys already done by reputable research organizations on similar issue within the period of this study.

The Summary Report Of The Interview At Nafdac

Under this section all information on NAFDAC as provided by the chief executive will be given, plus the summary of the interview conducted with the chief executive. As has been explained earlier, NAFDAC is fully called National Agency for Food and Drug Administration and Control. It was not at all easy to gain access into this government organization for the interviews mainly because of the very busy schedules of the chief executive coupled with the sensitive and risky nature of the job as well as the high need for security. This was not surprising at all because it was clear right from the onset that the nature of the interview falls under the category of elite interview and is known to be difficult because of the profiles and activities of the interviewees. Gaining access to such class of people normally would require a lot of contacts, connections and time of course. Beynon, H. (1988), argued that politics are involved, requiring the researcher in mediating power relationships and sometimes if not handled properly result in squeezing out the researcher. Gaining access to the chief executive of NAFDAC for the interview was a good experience that proved Beyon's argument to be reasonable. There was a lot of delays due mainly to the busy schedules and previous commitments of the chief executive. As a result of these the interview exercise was not carried out on time as planned earlier, however, it was a great relief that the breakthrough came at last.

It took series of contacts and arrangement that was started in Abuja, the Federal Capital, in July, 2003, to facilitate access to the chief executive of NAFDAC. The breakthrough finally came on the 30th of November, 2004, as the researcher could not take no for an answer, especially when there was strong conviction that a lot could be learnt from NAFDAC. The researcher was able to meet the Chief Executive of NAFDAC for the interview in her

Lagos office, because as had been explained earlier, this organization was chosen because it operates across the entire nation and reflects the national character which will likely make the outcome of the research on it to be reliable and applicable nationally. It has offices in the thirty- six states of the Federation and in Abuja, the Federal Capital, and provides jobs for all ethnic groups in Nigeria. On the day of the interview, however, as a result of the busy schedules of the chief executive, the researcher had to wait again for about two and half hours from 11.30 am to 2.00 pm at the waiting room before he was finally ushered in for the interview. It was a very long wait that paid off very well at last. The interview lasted from 2.00pm to about 4.30pm.

Brief Historical Development Of Nafdac

This is a Federal Government agency under the Federal Ministry of Health, responsible for the control and regulation of food, drugs, cosmetics and other regulated products in Nigeria. The current chief executive, Prof Dora N. Akunyili explained that under the directorate, the drug regulatory structure in Nigeria had most of the necessary components expected of a regulatory authority. According to her, prior to the establishment of NAFDAC, the Directorate of Food and Drug Administration and Control, in the Federal Ministry of Health was responsible for the control and regulation of food, drugs, cosmetics and other regulated products in Nigeria. She reported that there were drug laws but these were inefficient, and there were quality control laboratories as well. According to her provision for inspection, enforcement and even a fairly equipped drug-manufacturing laboratory were there. She however, stated that there was no product registration in place, and so, according to her, drug importation and manufacturing was a free for all affairs. Drug information and adverse drug reaction monitoring processes were not also in place and so there were no effective drug recall procedures.

According to her, the relatively well-developed regulatory process was thwarted by civil service bureaucracy, corruption, political instability and a host of other lapses. It was the efforts to remove these bottlenecks, and correct the lapses to ensure effectiveness that led to the establishment of NAFDAC by Decree No 15 of 1993 (as amended in 1999). The organization was then to control and regulate the manufacture, importation, exportation, distribution, advertisement, sale and use of food, drugs, cosmetics, chemicals/detergents, medical devices and all packaged drinks including the popular "pure water". According to her, the pioneer Director General of NAFDAC, Prof G.E. Osuide with his team was able to put in place a standard regulatory structure, which even Ghana used as a blueprint in establishing their Food and Drug Board. It was reported that today, Ghana does not have an elaborately established drug regulatory system as Nigeria, but they have a more effective regulation with the resultant low incidence of fake drugs. The researcher understood the above explanations to mean that despite the fact that Nigeria established elaborate drug regulatory system, it was not as effective as that of Ghana that was not elaborate, under the previous administration of Prof Osuide.

Nafdac As At 12Th Of April, 2001

As at 12th of April, 2001, when Prof Akunyili resumed as the new chief executive of NAFDAC, she reported that she was faced with an enormous task of reactivating a failed regulatory environment of over two decades. All these were as a result of the lapses stated above in section 5.1.1. According to her the situation has given rise to many negative trends and bad image for the country as follows:

-       Nigeria was rated as one of the countries with the highest incidence of fake and counterfeit drugs, and other unwholesome regulated products. As a result of this "made in Nigeria" drugs were officially unaccepted in other West African countries with strong regulations, e.g. Ghana, Sierra Leone and others.

-       Nigeria had the following types of fake drugs in   abundance:

-       Drugs with no active ingredient(s) e.g. having only   lactose or even chalk in capsules/tablets, olive oil in   Supradyn capsules;

-       Drugs with active ingredient(s) different from what Is   stated on the packages e.g. Paracetamol tabs packaged and labelled as Fansidar.

-       Drugs without full name and address of the manufacturer.

-       Clones of fast moving drugs.

-       Herbal preparations that are toxic or harmful or   ineffective or deceitfully mixed with orthodox medicine.

-       Expired drugs.

-      Drugs not certified and registered by NAFDAC.

According to her in addition to the above, local drug manufacturing was becoming unattractive in Nigeria due to unfair competition. This she said, resulted to many multinational companies divesting and leaving Nigeria out of frustration like Boehringer, ICI, Sandoz Merck, Boots and others. It is interesting to note here that the consequences of poor regulation also contributed negatively to the poor performance of the economy and increase in poverty due to loss of job by those that were working with the multinationals that were frustrated out of the country. This again is like a confirmation that effective organizations have a lot to contribute in the growth of the economy of the nation or the host nation where such organizations operate.

The chief executive of NAFDAC reported that the proliferation of fake and substandard products was not limited to drugs but includes expired products, and those without expiry dates or "Best Before" date or re-labelled with the intention of extending their shelf-life. It also includes non-iodised or insufficiently iodised salt; improperly processed and unregistered "pure water"; beer and other alcoholic drinks without "Best Before" date and alcohol content, and some were even of poor quality. She stated that most soft drinks marketed in Nigeria were of lower quality than similar brands marketed overseas, and that deceptively labeled juices became the fashion, and the example of such labeling include: "100% fruit juices, no sugar added, no added sweetener, no preservative, etc. and yet, juice from fruits that are not naturally very sweet like orange and guava were as sweet as honey, and these juices were actually regarded as classic drink within Nigerian environment." The other inadequacies she reported were that Nigerian bakers continued to use Potassium Bromate (as a bread enhancer), which was banned since the early 90s, for its implication in cancer, kidney failure, loss of hearing and breakdown of vitamins. She stated that staff morale in NAFDAC was low with general poor orientation and motivation, and that there was general poor public awareness on the problems of fake regulated products and the function of NAFDAC. This area was where she really made a great impact on the society that won her the support and respect of the Nigerian public. Her publicity strategies were superb and she effectively created the awareness that was not there before she took over the leadership of NAFDAC in April 2001. The other inadequacy she reported was the poor revenue collection and non-enforcement of sanctions due to general laxity and massive corruption which resulted to the agency being cash strapped and unable to carry out its functions as expected and authorized by law.

Implications Of Using Fake Drugs And Other Substandard Products

The chief executive of NAFDAC was so committed to the tasks before her that she described faking/counterfeiting especially, drug faking as the greatest evil of our time and the highest weapon of terrorism against public health, as well as an act of economic sabotage. She said that it was an ill wind that blows nobody good, and that the evil of fake drugs was worse than the combined scourge of malaria, HIV/AIDS and armed robbery put together. She added that the social problem posed by hard drugs like cocaine or heroine cannot even be compared with the damage done by fake drugs, because illicit drugs are taken out of choice and by those that can afford them. She was of the opinion that fake drugs have led to treatment failures, killed many, embarrassed Nigerian healthcare providers, eroded the confidence of the public on the healthcare delivery system and destroyed the local industries that were facing unfair competition.

Factors Responsible For The Current Changes And Successes At Nafdac

The chief executive of NAFDAC was asked to give some hints on what was responsible for her successful leadership at NAFDAC. She was asked to specifically explain the reasons for her outstanding success and the operation of a more effective regulatory system, when according to her, the regulatory process was in the past thwarted by civil service bureaucracy, corruption and political instability. In view of the fact that it was impossible for NAFDAC to perform in the past few years when there were uncontrolled massive importation of fake drugs and expired food products all over the country, she was also asked to highlight the strengths for the changes that made the success possible.

She started the response to the above questions by saying that the followers are not fools and that they will not trust the leader if they have no reason for the trust. She said that integrity is the number one strength. She went further to explain that the leader must be consistently honest, transparent and sincere, and that with these the leader can easily influence and command the respect of the followers and that this has been her experience at NAFDAC. The views of the chief executive of NAFDAC here is a sort of confirmation of what Adair (1983) stated about integrity which Viscount Slim defined as the quality which makes people trust you. It appears clearly here that the issue of trust can never be over-emphasized when it comes to commanding the respect of the followers and having influence over them, which is the sine qua non of leadership (Northouse 2001). Northouse said that without influence, leadership does not exist and this seems to be in line with this emerging evidence in Nigeria. This also goes to show that there may not be any contextual barriers after all, to the effects of the leader's integrity on the followers or subordinates anywhere in the world. Kouzes and Posner (2002) stated that it is clear that if people anywhere are to willingly follow someone (whether it be into battle or into the boardroom, the front office or the front lines) they first want to assure themselves that the person is worthy of their trust. They want to know that the person is truthful, ethical, and principled. They arrived at this conclusion after years of conducting studies on leadership, internationally, from 1980s, and in every survey they conducted, honesty has been selected more often than any other leadership characteristics, and overall, it emerges as the single most important ingredient in the leader-constituent relationship. They stated that when people talk to them about the qualities they admire in leaders, they often use "integrity" and "character" as synonymous with honesty. It can therefore be said that the integrity of the leader is a strong factor for successful leadership especially in organizations, anywhere in the world. Kouzes and Posner (2002) stated that a leader with integrity has one self, at home and at work, with family and with colleagues. They added that leaders without integrity are putting on an act.

The chief executive of NAFDAC further explained that leaders can instil fear on the subordinate to make them afraid, but being afraid of the leader is not the same thing as respecting the leader and that this does not give the desired results. According to her, whenever the workers become afraid of the leader they will give eye service which does not promote productivity. The subordinates may not respect the leader if they do not trust him or her due to double standard. In other words, the respect is to be earned by the leader through his or her consistently upright, transparent, and honest conducts, as rightly observed by the subordinates. She said that eye service does not show genuine commitment to duties. She added that workers watch carefully to know whether the boss have double standard or not, and that they are usually smart in peeping into the affairs of the boss to establish whether there is double standard or hidden agenda. This therefore means that leaders with skeleton in their cupboards cannot succeed in hiding them from their subordinates for too long, because they will eventually find out through their networks. According to her experience in NAFDAC, workers would easily give their support and trust the leader once they establish that there is no double standard and that the leader has integrity and is upright and trustworthy.

Re-Orientation And Motivation Of Nafdac Staff For Greater Commitment

The Director-General of NAFDAC was asked to explain why there was high level of commitment and motivation amongst almost all the staff of the organization under her, and she explained that it was due mainly to re-orientation and the incentives her administration put in place. She said that the inevitable need for staff re-orientation was glaring when she took over and her administration needed total change of fixed mindset and in fact, an organizational cultural revolution. Through numerous interactions, according to her, she was able to communicate to the staff of NAFDAC that theirs is a call to a mission of which they could not afford to fail because of the obvious consequences, of pain, suffering, and death for them, and their loved ones. According to her she was able to rub it into them that for things to turn around in NAFDAC they must run the agency in a business-like manner but not as a private enterprise. She also communicated to them in clear terms that she was prepared to work with those willing to change from their old ways and would not hesitate to flush out the bad eggs.

The NAFDAC boss explained that staff discipline, motivation and general welfare were seriously addressed. Accordingly, she took some measures to reposition staff for better effectiveness such as:

-       The retrenchment of corrupt, redundant and incorrigible   staff;

-       Induction training for new staff, specialized in-house and   overseas training and computer appreciation courses were   organized, and information technology tools were made available;

-     Effective delegation of duties and staff empowerment;

-     Adequate reward for heroic activities;

-     Leadership by example;

Constant staff performance monitoring to ensure commitment and effectiveness. To encourage good staff, hard work, dedication and transparency, are adequately compensated while any form of laxity or corruption is severely sanctioned. She said that when hard work and integrity are not recognized and rewarded, corruption and ineptitude are promoted.

She said that the open reward system was adopted when she took over the leadership. According to her, the adopted system makes it possible for staff to be rewarded openly for any outstanding achievement, and the system equally provides for punishment for laxity or any act of corruption and shady deals. She gave the example of how a member staff that was just three months in the agency was instantly rewarded and sent overseas for further training when he performed a heroic task of single handedly causing the arrest of a fake drug importer who had successfully cleared the imported fake drugs and had loaded these out of the port already. Due to high motivation for result achievement and commitment to the goals and mission of the organization, the young man took the risk and demobilized the vehicle by puncturing the tyres of the vehicle conveying the fake drugs and ran away to report the case to armed agency staff who effected the arrest.

She made it clear that under her administration, NAFDAC established an open system that encourages team spirit and transparency. They operate what she explained as: "watch me I watch you". This she said exposes every member of staff to scrutiny by other staff, and this way it is difficult for any staff to indulge in corrupt practices or bribe taking. According to her, staff were encouraged to expose any big company involved in any shady deal of importing expired products or fakes into the country with a reward for promotion. She said that this strategy has helped NAFDAC to catch one of the big multinationals operating in Nigeria, and the woman who caught the company was promoted to Director level. The arrest of the big multinational was indeed a surprising eye-opener, to NAFDAC, that even the respected multinational who is supposed to be the model that sets good standard of operation, could turn to be part of the problems of Nigerian environment by importing expired products that can be harmful into the country. This was like a case of double standard by the multinational known for high standard of quality, and very good care for human lives generally. This unexpected behaviour may need further studies to gain some useful insights on the causes.

The NAFDAC boss made it clear that they do not only take care of good performance by instant reward, but that they also reward laxity by dismissal. According to her all shady deals and cases of corruption are dealt with adequately through suspension and dismissals. She gave example of a relation of hers who was involved in such case but was not spared of the appropriate punishment which was termination of appointment. She said that this particular case was a very big test case for her and eventually earned her a good credit because it made her staff to believe in her and to give her their total trust, support and respect. One cannot but see this as a very good case of leadership by example and will therefore agree completely with her views that the fundamental thing in leadership is leading by example. This makes the staff or subordinates to trust the leader and when they trust, according to her, they work out their hearts, and when they do not, they do eye service.

Acquisition Of Leadership Abilities

The chief executive of NAFDAC was asked to explain how she acquired her leadership abilities and she said that it was through upbringing, training and religion. She added that it was the combination of all, and that what is important is to be determined, work hard and have enough knowledge of the task to be able to grasp what is happening. She summarized that it can be said to be a combination of acquisition of abilities partly by birth and partly by learning. In other words, her views on leadership abilities or what can be called traits, or abilities she exhibits, are very much in agreement with the arguments of Kirkpatrick and Locke (1991) who postulated that leaders differ from non- leaders on six traits such as drive, the desire to lead, honesty and integrity, self-confidence, cognitive ability, and knowledge of the business. They argued that individuals can be born with these traits, and they can learn them or both, and these were the views expressed by the NAFDAC boss, and incidentally this has been the line of thought of this research exercise. Just like Kirkpatrick and Locke argued, it can be said that people are born with some talent or ability and that is why it can be said that some are extrovert in nature and some are introvert. Some are naturally very brilliant and some simply display low level intelligence. Some improve on their level of knowledge and intelligence through continuous learning. This same argument can therefore be extended to the issue of leadership ability. Some people as have been argued display leadership ability right from birth without much training, while some improve and acquire leadership ability and skills through learning. The statement of the chief executive of NAFDAC is a confirmation and strong support for our argument that leaders can be born and can also be made through training.

Factors Militating Against Effective Food And Drug

Regulation In Nigeria

Professor Akunyili reported that faking and dumping of drugs and other regulated products into Nigeria were ab initio caused by weak regulation and all the directors and immediate subordinates interviewed confirmed this. She said that some of the factors that weakened the regulatory functions were:

Corruption and Poor orientation of workers

According to her corruption is a driving force for poor regulation, which encourages drug faking/counterfeiting. As a result of this the efficiency of personnel is adversely affected by corruption and conflict of interests, resulting in laws not being enforced, and criminals not being arrested and prosecuted. She said that criminals were having a field day because they have found that the counterfeiting of medicines is financially lucrative and of relatively low risk compared with smuggling narcotics and running of weapons. They have therefore shifted from the smuggling of narcotics and running of weapons to counterfeiting of medicines, and this was part of what made Nigerian situation pathetic. At the inception of her administration therefore, the NAFDAC staff she inherited were not spared of the cankerworm called corruption. According to her they had very poor orientation, fixed retrogressive mind-set, they indulged in over-sampling (collecting unreasonable large quantities of samples for analysis), wilful delay in registration processes, and on the part of the importers, dumping was business as usual as long as they could pay their way through the regulatory authorities.

According to her some local producers did not pay too much attention to their "Good Manufacturing Practice (GMP) and the quality of their products. This she reported was partly as a result of inadequate supervision on the part of NAFDAC due to negative attitude to work and corruption. She also stated that distributors were not spared of these corruptive tendencies because some of them were involved in re-labelling of expired drugs and other regulated products with the intention of extending their shelf life. She however, stated that they were happy that all these ugly practices have been drastically reduced to pave way for fake drug eradication and creation of a strong regulatory environment, through their efforts and fight against corruption. The ability to deal with the ugly situation and the subsequent creation of a strong regulatory environment is not a mean achievement and should be attributed to the leadership ability of the chief executive who demonstrated great courage in tackling the menace.

Inadequate Cooperation from Government Agencies

The NAFDAC chief executive reported that the absence of teamwork among the various sectors of government (NAFDAC, Customs, Nigerian Drugs Law Enforcement Agency, Standard Organization of Nigeria and Nigerian Shipping Lines and others) creates a fertile ground for counterfeiters to escape detection, arrest and sanctions. As a result of this, some of the criminally minded importers take advantage of this lack of cooperation to propagate their illegal business. According to her, in the past, 'Stop Notices' issued by NAFDAC to some of these Agencies at the ports had been ignored or not acted on, resulting to products suspected to be fake, substandard or unwholesome being released into the markets.

Unfavourable Government Policies

The NAFDAC boss reported the Nigerian Port Reforms Policy of 1996 by the government as a typical example of an unfavourable government policy, which denied NAFDAC access to the ports of entry, thereby promoting easy influx of fake/counterfeit products into the country unchecked. She reported that this situation existed from 1996 until October 2001 when the present administration changed the policy and returned NAFDAC inspectors to the entry ports. This is indeed a typical example of where poor government policy can be changed by a committed chief executive through consistent argument and presentation of facts by the affected stakeholder. It can also be said that trust and confidence in the chief executive mission and goals may have also facilitated the desired change that brought back NAFDAC inspectors back to the entry ports. This is a sort of indicator that the government may likely listen to a superior argument and be ready to change some policies if convinced that good results will come out of it, as was in this case.

Other Factors

She stated other factors that were militating against effective food and drug regulation in Nigeria as:

-       False declaration by importers;

-       Insecure and unfriendly environment;

-       Discriminating regulations by exporting countries;

-       Sophistication in clandestine drug manufacture;

-       Inadequate funding;

-       Lack of inadequate legislation;

-       Chaotic drug distribution system;

-       Poor database on health related activities;

-       Poor rational use of drugs;

-       Ignorance and poor public awareness;

-       Illegal and deceitful advertisement; and

-       Demand exceeding supply.

All the above factors were what the NAFDAC chief executive

gave as the militating factors against effective food and drug regulation in Nigeria and one can say that from the assessment of the current situation she has fought very hard to bring them under control. She has demonstrated the ability of facing challenges and turning bad situation around, and this can only be attributed to good leadership.

The Rebuilding Of Nafdac

The NAFDAC boss reported that when the new management came on board, the appalling state of the organization was an emergency that demanded urgent attention and she was under a lot of pressure. According to her, she transformed the pressure into a positive drive to turn around the system for the better, which she passed on to the staff through various meetings and interactions. She stated that the interactive meetings revealed a number of human and communication problems, top of which was low perception of the Agency's mission and responsibility to public health by staff. She added that they were well-qualified civil servants with long years of experience, and that most of them had moved from the Federal Ministry of Health to start the Agency in 1993. She therefore said that it was natural for many of them to resist any form of change from the status quo, even though the need for change was inevitable. From her experience she cautioned that in initiating change, it is important to bear in mind that there must be some resistance. In the case of NAFDAC, she said that the resistance came in form of "we started the Agency, this is not how we do thing here." This again is an example of how human beings can resist change even if the change is for good as it turned out to be in this case, and that people like to remain the way they are and maintain the status quo. Despite the resistance to the inevitable changes the NAFDAC boss was able to put the relevant changes in place in the various forms as stated below, to move the organization forward.

a) Staff Rationalization and Recruitment

The chief executive of NAFDAC reported that at the inception of her administration, there was a basic problem with staff posting which was not originally based on qualification and that led to ineptitude and subsequent inability of staff to fulfill their functions and so the rebuilding of NAFDAC has to start with staff rationalization. According to her, team of consultants, were therefore invited to reposition staff according to qualification and area of competence. New recruitments were also carried out through very meticulous and effective screening exercises involving external consultants and experts. Directors of NAFDAC also interviewed confirmed that these steps were taken.

b) Restructuring of NAFDAC

After putting the right people in place the chief executive was faced with the real challenge of team consolidation, and her next line of action was to restructure the Agency for better effectiveness. As a result of this, the organization was restructured into eight functional directorates as against the previous six. According to her the two new directorates created were the Ports Inspectorate and Enforcement and were meant to further position the agency to effectively tackle the problems emanating from inspection lapses and poor enforcement activities that were the most critical problem areas.

Presently, there are six (6) Technical and two (2) Services Directorates in the Agency namely:-

-       Laboratory Services

-       Narcotics and Controlled Substances

-       Enforcement

- Port Inspection

- Establishment Inspection

- Registration and Regulatory Affairs

- Administration and Finance (A&F)

- Planning, Research and Statistics.

In addition, according to her, ten state offices were established, and the existing twenty-six were strengthened to cover the thirty-six states and Abuja. Six zonal offices were put in place to coordinate the activities of the state offices, and three special inspectorate offices were established in the three towns with the biggest drug market (Onitsha, Aba and Kano).

She also reported that NAFDAC has four laboratories in Lagos (Oshodi and Yaba), Kaduna and Maiduguri, but that unfortunately the Oshodi laboratory was in October, 2002, vandalized after it had been refurbished and equipped. This therefore necessitated another round of refurbishing and re-equipping. She stated that the Yaba laboratory is now well equipped and accredited by both WHO (World Health Organization) and European Union (EU). According to her the old laboratories both in Kaduna and Maiduguri were being re-equipped and new ones were being built in the South-South and South-East, and that the aim of building laboratories in every zone was to facilitate product testing and to decongest the existing ones. In addition to these, new warehouses, land border offices were constructed, and portakabins in all the ports serving as cheap but effective offices.

The NAFDAC boss reported that about six months after assumption of office, she was fortunate to have on board a Chairman and Members of Council who shared her passion for NAFDAC and were convinced that she was in the right track and therefore lent all necessary support, which was sustained till date.

She reported that her management team was encouraged by the Council to organize a retreat for both Council and Management (Directors and Deputy Directors) of the Agency, where they rubbed minds together, formulated and shared the new Vision, Mission and Goal. According to her they created a good and relaxed opportunity to share strategic plans of each director-ate. There is no doubt that all these helped the chief executive of NAFDAC to achieve the outstanding results within the short space of time. She built strong team spirit and all the subordin-ates interviewed confirmed this and were happy to be part of the team that made NAFDAC what it has become. She got the board to agree to support the strategies and goals of the man-agement team, and by this she pre-emptied possible conflicts from the board. There is a lot to learn from her approach by other leaders in organization, especially those in government organizations.

c) NAFDAC Vision, Mission and Goal

She reported that the new Management of NAFDAC resolved that fake drugs, unwholesome food and other substandard regu-lated products must be brought to the barest minimum in the shortest possible time. As a result of this they needed a clear cut vision, set goal and strategies, and so the organization came up with the following:

VISION: "To safeguard public health"

MISSION: "To safeguard public health by ensuring that only the right quality products are manufactured, imported, exported, advertised, distributed, sold and used"

CURRENT GOAL: "Is to eradicate fake drugs and other substand-ard regulated Products"

d) Review of NAFDAC Tariff

The NAFDAC tariff was last reviewed in 1994 according to the chief executive, and she felt that this was out of tune with the present economic realities. As a result of this the management embarked on upward review of the tariff in December, 2001, in order to be able to deal with the following:

Increased operational cost such as the 1600% increase in diesel from 1994, and the need to acquire modern equipment or service old ones for better effectiveness, and ensure adequate supplies of high-grade analytical chemicals.

Need to increase analytical/testing parameters to conform with international standard.

Encourage local manufacturers by creating a differential tariff between local and imported products. For example Ethical drug registration is two hundred and fifty thousand Naira (N250,000), while locally produced is fifty thousand Naira (N50,000).

Sponsor staff to inspect production facilities outside Nigeria at no additional cost to the importer.

e) Review of Laws/Reconstitution of the Legal Unit

The NAFDAC boss reported that Nigerian Government has enacted many laws and promulgated many decrees to combat faking/counterfeiting of drugs, foods and other regulated products. These laws unfortunately were weak according to her, and non-deterrent, and some were unimplementable, but NAFDAC still derives its authority from them. She said that the weaknesses in the laws were not as bad as the lack of will to enforce them. For example the Federal and State Task Forces first established by Decree 21 of 1988, now existing under Decree 25 of 1999, which served as the enforcement arm of NAFDAC, suffered from a background of corruption and continual change of leadership. As a result the activities of the task forces lacked credibility and continuity, and any progress made could not be sustained, at the same time the fake drug criminals were taking advantage of easily obtainable court injunctions and court orders to stop NAFDAC from carrying out the sanctions.

As pointed out by her some of the existing laws clearly show their inherent non-deterrent capacities as shown below:

Decree No. 35 of 1974 (amended by Food and Drug Act Cap 150 of 1990) provides for a fine of N1,000 for offenders (producers and importers of fake and unwholesome drugs and other NAFDAC regulated products). This was reviewed upward in the Decree 21 of 1995 to N50,000, which is still not deterrent enough.

NAFDAC Decree NO. 15 of 1993 has a penalty of N5,000 for obstructing an officer from entering suspicious premises.

However, the outdated laws were reviewed and have since been sent to the National Assembly to be enacted into law. According to her, in the interim the regulatory process has been strengthened, by putting in place some administrative guidelines within the law. Also put in place, were the strategy and framework for preparing and drafting regulations, which will provide legal and technical details for protection of the Agency. Based on the NAFDAC experience, she strongly recommends that organizations should strive to perform their functions irrespective of any constraint, by exploiting their potentials in expanding existing administrative capacities.

The chief executive of NAFDAC highlighted the inherent non-deterrent capacities of the existing laws, using the examples of: Decree No. 35 of 1974 (amended by Food and Drug Act Cap 150 of 1990) which provides for a fine of N,1000 for offenders (producers and importers of fake and unwholesome drugs and other NAFDAC regulated products). She reported that this was reviewed upwards in the Decree 21 of 1995 to fifty thousand Naira

(N50,000), and was still not deterrent enough.

NAFDAC Decree No. 15 of 1993 has a penalty of five thousand Naira (N,5000) for obstructing an officer from entering suspicious premises.

She therefore reported that the outdated laws were reviewed and have since been sent to the National Assembly to be enacted into law and that NAFDAC has put in place, the strategy and framework for preparing and drafting regulations, which will provide legal and technical details for protection of the Agency. Based on her experience in NAFDAC she highly recommend that organizations should strive to perform their functions irrespective of any constraint, by exploiting their potentials in expanding existing administrative capacities.

f) Guidelines and Standard Operating Procedures (SOPs)

New SOPs were developed for all the divisions of various Directorates with special emphasis on Registration/ Regulatory Affairs, Inspectorate, Laboratory Services and Narcotics/Control Substances Directorates.

-	The overall boss also reported that new guidelines	were developed to cover:

-	Registration of locally manufactured and imported food, drugs (including vaccines, biologicals and herbals) and other regulated products.

-	Exportation and importation or regulated products.

	Issuance of Narcotics and Controlled Substances	permit.

She stated that the new guidelines were quite comprehensive and have improved communication between the stakeholders and the Agency while the SOP have reduced decision-making time in registration procedures, thereby eliminating unnecessary bottlenecks that existed in the past.

g) Enlightenment Campaigns

The researcher reported earlier while justifying the selection of NAFDAC as one of the organizations to be studied, that the current chief executive of NAFDAC had made a tremendous impact on the Nigerian public through effective public enlightenment. This was one of the factors that made her and the activities of the organization popular. She created good awareness and the public became aware of the consequences of fake drug and supported the fight against it. The new Management of NAFDAC under the leadership of Prof. Dora Akunyili, was able to analyse the past interventions to enforce regulation in Nigeria, and arrived at the conclusion that they were rather ad-hoc measures, and as such, their impacts, if any, was not sustainable. The Management therefore decided that there was need for a review of the strategy. In the past, NAFDAC spent all its energies as well as its meager resources in prosecuting hundreds of cases, which often turned out to be endless and frustrating. The Management consequently deemed it more effective to embark on massive enlightenment campaign, dialogue, education and persuasion in their regulatory activities because this strategy addressed the fundamental issue at stake, which according to them is behavioural change. As a participant observer it is easy to confirm that massive awareness was created through various media and this worked and made the public to be fully aware and to support the activities of NAFDAC. The campaign was further carried to the level of secondary school students via essay competitions that depicts the ill effects of fake drugs. According to the chief executive of the organization, this level of awareness ensures the future protection of the populace because of the indelible impression on the mind of these younger ones.

She added that the Agency's Food and Drug Information Center (FDIC) was strengthened with enough manpower and information technology to constantly inform the public of their activities and other important alert notices through their quarterly publication of the Agency's bulletin and their bi-monthly newspaper publications of differences between identified fake products and the genuine ones. According to her these methods were meant to involve the public and all stakeholders in the business of safeguarding public health. Enlightenment and the resultant voluntary change of heart, she said, are result-oriented and complimentary to confrontation and prosecution, which the Agency had used over the years with little or no fruits. She said that it was the co-operation and support of the Chairman and members of Onitsha Medicine Dealers Association, brought about by NAFDAC enlightenment campaign, that enabled them to locate Marcel Nnakwe's warehouses, seize the drugs, got him sign a letter of forfeiture of these drugs for destruction and also made him to apologize to the good people of the country.

The interview with the NAFDAC chief executive was a very rewarding experience and very useful in this study because at every stage the researcher was able to observe effective leadership in action. It was a good opportunity to compare theory with practice in the field. There is no doubt that Professor Dora Akunyili has proved herself to be an effective leader with integrity based on all the evidence around her and the confirmations from direct and indirect stakeholders. The tables and exhibits under appendices 4 and 5 speak volumes in support of an effective leader with high level of integrity.

Analysis And Discussions Of Data

This section is devoted to analysis and discussions of data collected through the perceived leader integrity scale (PLIS) of Craig and Gustafson (1998), the questionnaires, interviews, and secondary data, all relating to the studies carried out in the successful NAFDAC as mentioned above. All the analysis are geared towards answering all the research questions and proving the hypothesis that are all focused on leadership with integrity. The effective analysis of these data and satisfactory answers to all the research questions will help us to advance the argument and relate specific trait like integrity to the leadership outcome like productivity or growth of the organizations. Ultimately it will be possible to see the effects of these analysed data on the trait theory which suggests that organization will work better if the people in managerial positions have designated leadership profiles, especially from the Nigerian context. The summary of the findings are presented as the data analysis progresses. In this chapter the discussions and analysis relate to the findings and data collected from the National Agency for Food and Drug Administration and Control (NAFDAC). The discussions and analysis of the data from Neimeth International Pharmaceuticals Plc are covered separately in chapter six below.

Confirmation Of Integrity As Vital Leadership Trait In Nafdac

The first relevant research question here is Research Question 1 – Can the integrity of the chief executive of the organization be confirmed by the immediate subordinates in the same organization? The corresponding hypothesis is Hypothesis 1 – The immediate subordinates of a chief executive that has integrity, will notice it, feel the impact of it, and can testify to it. The other relevant questions under this are research questions 2 and 4, and the corresponding hypothesis is 2 and 4.

The Perceived Leadership Integrity Scale (PLIS) of Craig and Gustafson (1998) is used here to find answer to the research question 1 and others. This instrument measures subordinates' perceptions of their leaders' integrity in organizational settings. The process requires summing up of all responses on the 31 statements (see appendix 2 for details). The lowest and best score is expected to be 31, and indicates that the leader is perceived to be highly ethical, which means high level of integrity. The maximum score on the other hand is expected to be 124, and this will indicate that the leader is perceived to be of low ethical. There are three ranges as follows:

$$31 - 35 \quad \text{High ethical;}$$

$$36 - 66 \quad \text{Moderate;}$$

$$67 - 124 \quad \text{Low ethical.}$$

NAFDAC Data Analysis

In answering research question 1, using the above standard and format (PLIS), the questionnaires that were completed by the immediate subordinates to the chief executive at NAFDAC were summarized and analysed as shown below in table 5.2., for the answer to research question 1.

Table 5.2: Summary Scores for PLIS in NAFDAC

Subordinates	1	2	3	4	5	Total	Average
Scores	31	31	33	35	39	169	33.8

Out of eight immediate subordinates, five completed the questionnaires given to them. Two out of the five scored the chief executive 31 each, in other words they gave her highest score possible on integrity. Another subordinate scored her 33, and the fourth subordinate scored her 35. All these four subordinates scores came within the range of 31- 35, which is high ethical and reliable confirmation that the chief executive is highly ethical and therefore has high integrity. The fifth subordinate scored her 39, which is within the range of moderate. Altogether the range was found to be from 31 to 39, and summed up on individual basis the average was found to be 33.8. Therefore the immediate subordinates rating of the chief executive of NAFDAC could be said to fall within the range of 31 – 35. In line with the above ranges, the chief executive of NAFDAC could be said to be of high ethical generally. It could therefore be said that she has high level of integrity going by the assessments of her immediate subordinates. It could also be said that hypothesis 1, has been proved right in NAFDAC. In other words, the immediate subordinate of the chief executive with genuine integrity have observed and felt the impact, and could testify to it. Based on these findings and confirmations of the immediate subordinates of the chief executive of NAFDAC, it could be said that she has high level of integrity.

Further Analysis Of The Data For Answers To Research Question 2

Further analysis and answers to research questions 2 are provided, using interview data and secondary data as well as the PLIS as they relate to NAFDAC. The research question 2 is therefore restated: Is there any evidence that the chief executive of the successful organization under investigation has high level of integrity? The corresponding hypothesis (Hypothesis 2) states: The success of the organization and the confirmation of the immediate subordinates will show that the chief executive of the investigated successful organization has high level of integrity.

The analysis already done has provided answers for research question 2 already. The immediate subordinates in NAFDAC averagely scored their chief executive very high on integrity. The five immediate subordinates in NAFDAC gave average score of 33.8 which falls within the range of 31 – 35 (high ethical). These stand for high level of integrity, and so it can logically be said that there is evidence that the chief executive of NAFDAC has high level of integrity. Further analysis and answering of the questions were carried out below, using the interview data and the secondary data obtained from NAFDAC.

NAFDAC Interview Data Analysis

During the interview with the chief executive at NAFDAC, a lot of statements and responses from the chief executive on some of the interview questions could also provide answers to research questions 2. The statements and responses portrayed the chief executive to be of high integrity and very instrumental to the positive changes and increase in productivity and improved performance of the organization. For example she was specifically asked to explain the reasons for the current changes and outstanding successes and operation of a more effective regulatory system that was impossible before April, 2001 at NAFDAC. She started the response to the above questions as follows:

"The followers are not fools, they will not trust the leader if they have no reason for the trust. Integrity is the number one strength. The leader must be consistently honest, transparent and sincere, and with these the leader can easily influence and command the respect of the followers and this has been the experience at NAFDAC."

The views of the chief executive of NAFDAC here is a sort of confirmation of what Adair (1983) stated about integrity which Viscount Slim defined as the quality which makes people trust you. It is also very much in agreement with Kouzes and Posner (2002) argument which states that it is clear that if people anywhere are to willingly follow someone (whether it be into battle or into the boardroom, the front office or the front lines) they first want to assure themselves that the person is worthy of their trust.

During the interview the NAFDAC boss reported that when her new management came on board, the appalling state of the organization was an emergency that demanded urgent attention and she was under a lot of pressure. According to her, she transformed the pressure into a positive drive to turn around the system for the better, which she passed on to the staff through various meetings and interactions. She reported that some of the factors that earlier weakened the regulatory functions were corruptions and poor orientations of workers amongst others. She made it clear that corruption was a driving force for poor regulation which encourages drug faking/counterfeiting. From her point of view the NAFDAC staff she inherited were not spared of the cankerworm called corruption. "They had very poor orientation, fixed retrogressive mind-set, and indulged in over-sampling, and willful delay in registration process." For her to have turned around the corrupt system for the better, is another evidence that she has high level of integrity otherwise the turnaround would not have been possible. This is also an evidence that the increase in productivity as shown above in the various activities tables and the improved performance of the organization, have something to do with the integrity of the chief executive.

The NAFDAC boss made it clear during the interview that they do not only take care of good performance by instant reward, but that they also reward laxity and corruption by dismissal at NAFDAC. According to her, "all shady deals and cases of corruption are dealt with adequately through suspension and dismissals irrespective of who is involved." She gave example of her brother-in-law who as a staff of NAFDAC was involved in a case of corruption, but was not spared of the appropriate punishment which was termination of appointment. She went on to say:

"This particular case was a very big test case for me but I had to choose between doing the right thing and saving my brother-in-law's job. This to me was a serious test on leadership by example. I had no better choice than to terminate the appointment of my brother-in-law according to the standing rules because everybody was waiting to see if I had double standard. This was not so pleasant for me because it brought strained relationship within the family but it had to be done because as a leader I have a duty to lead by example."

According to the chief executive, the bold decision to lead by example was what eventually earned her outstanding credit because it made her staff to believe in her and to give her their total trust, support and respect. They all saw her as a leader with integrity that should be trusted and supported at all cost because she did what corrupt leaders would not do. This according to her made her leadership job much easier.

During the interview the chief executive of NAFDAC emphasized the inevitable need for staff re-orientation and the efforts made so far for total change of mind-set as well as an organizational cultural revolution. She explained that her administration established an open system that encourages team spirit and transparency. She said:

"We operate what is known as: 'watch me I watch you'. This exposes every member of staff to scrutiny by other staff, and this way it is difficult for any staff to indulge in corrupt practices or bribe taking."

According to her, members of staff were encouraged to expose any big company involved in any shady deal of importing expired products or fakes into the country with a reward for promotion. She said that this strategy has helped NAFDAC to catch one of the big multinationals operating in Nigeria, and the woman who caught the company was promoted to director level. She went further to explain.

"To encourage good staff, hard work, dedication and transparency, are adequately compensated while any form of laxity or corruption is severely sanctioned. When hard work and integrity are not recognized and rewarded, corruption and ineptitude are promoted."

A critical consideration of this strategy of transparency and recognition and reward for integrity, as well as promotion of team spirit can be convincing about the high level of integrity and commitment of the chief executive to lead by example. It shows that she is open to scrutiny just like others because she approved and supported the open system. This again is evidence that the chief executive of NAFDAC has high level of integrity. During the interview she was asked to explain how she acquired the leadership ability, and in response she said:

"It was through upbringing, training and religion. It was the combination of all, and what is important is to be determined, work hard and have enough knowledge of the task to be able to grasp what is happening. It can be said to be a combination of acquisition of abilities partly by birth and partly by learning."

The response above revealed some useful points about the acquisition of leadership ability or possession of traits. The NAFDAC boss views are very much in agreement with the arguments of Kirkpatrick and Locke (1991) who argued that individuals can be born with leadership traits, and they can learn them or both. The researcher has also expressed the views that leaders can be born or made and this has been the line of thought of this research exercise. It is therefore interesting and encouraging to note that this exemplary leader from the practical point of view supports this argument. It can therefore be right to say that training also helped her to achieve this success. Based on this it could be said that effective leaders can be made through training and development.

NAFDAC Secondary Data Analysis

Reviews of some of the publications by NAFDAC have been quite revealing and very much in agreement with responses and views expressed by the boss during the interview. For example, a paper presentation by the chief executive of NAFDAC as a guest speaker at the Lagos Business School Breakfast Club Meeting held on the 6th July, 2004, was titled "Public Sector Performance – The Case of NAFDAC". In the opening remarks the chief executive stated that she was happy to share her experience in NAFDAC with others in order to encourage them that with the right spirit, any moribund system can be revived.

She went further to say that it is easier to build a new house than to rebuild a collapsed one, and that in the same vein it is easier to build an organization from the scratch than to revive a failed system. She stated:

"It was an arduous task turning NAFDAC around, but despite all the difficulties encountered in the task of evolving a new NAFDAC, we were convinced that with determination and hard work we will succeed, and we are succeeding."

She added that performance in any sector depends on the people and on the will to do what is right by putting service to God and humanity above personal gains. She further explained that the revival of NAFDAC activities and the change in attitude of stakeholders after over two decades of poor regulation could not have happened without attitudinal change of staff and stakeholders. She further stated:

"The sheer determination to succeed through hard work, honesty, transparency and the total unalloyed commitment on the part of staff of the Agency, made the rebirth of NAFDAC possible, and this has translated to better regulation and control."

The first and the greatest of the achievements and gains cited in the paper is the institution of a culture that promotes transparency, accountability and hard work in NAFDAC, which abhors corruption. It was clearly stated that this brought about a behavioural change in the staff of the Agency and is the oil that lubricated the wheel of the work to success.

All the above can be said to be strong evidence that the organization has had over two decades of poor regulation and that the influence of the current chief executive brought about the positive change that made the outstanding success and progress possible. Bryman (1992) defined leadership in terms of process of social influence whereby a leader steers members of a group towards a goal, and it could be said that the influence of the

NAFDAC leader has been outstanding. It could also be said that without the institution of a culture that promotes transparency, accountability and hard work in NAFDAC, which abhors corruption, the rebirth would not have been possible. This could be strong evidence that the increase in productivity and improved performance of NAFDAC has something to do with the integrity of the chief executive. Kane (2006) stated that effective and enlightened leaders live in integrity even when it is challenging. This seems to have been well demonstrated by the NAFDAC chief executive, because she has been able to create willingness in people to trust and follow her despite the difficult and challenging state of the Agency she inherited. The invitation to the chief executive to come and share her experience with other chief executives at the Lagos Business School Breakfast Club Meeting could be seen as evidence that organizations in the same environment have noticed and acknowledged the outstanding success recorded by the new NAFDAC under the leadership of Professor Dora Akunyili.

The chief executive of NAFDAC cited the institution of a culture that promotes transparency, accountability and hard work in NAFDAC as the greatest of the achievements and gains. This is another confirmation that the chief executive has high regard for integrity, and that the increase in productivity and improved performance in the organization has a lot to do with the integrity of the chief executive. It is necessary to add here that NAFDAC chief executive has proved that she is a woman of high integrity ever before she joined NAFDAC in 2001. She proved her worth in PTF (Petroleum Trust Fund) her former place of work. It was widely reported that she got the present appointment in NAFDAC as a result of the legacy she left behind in PTF. The report stated that as an officer of PTF she was sick and was officially sent overseas for medical treatment, but on getting to the overseas hospital it was discovered that she did not need the operation. On learning this she demanded that the fund approved for her treatment should be returned to Nigerian government. The foreign medical personnel, according to the report, found her attitude to the fund strange and un-Nigerian judging from the attitudes of others they have witnessed in the past, but she insisted despite all advice to the contrary. The money was returned to PTF and this single act earned her a commendation letter from the overall boss of PTF. Her outstanding act of integrity at PTF was what earned her the respect, and later the big job at NAFDAC.

The other achievements she cited in her paper that could easily be verified and confirmed by other stakeholders are restated below as she puts them:

-    "The production capacities of our local   pharmaceutical industries have increased tremendously according to reports by individual manufacturers and the Pharmaceutical Manufacturers Group of the Manufacturers Association of Nigeria (PMG-MAN).

-    GlaxoSmithkline recorded a 77% growth in sales, which the General Manager West Africa   attributed to, "NAFDAC living up to its responsibilities of enforcing strict compliance   to product regulation". (The Guardian Newspaper, 29th January 2003, P.45).

-    May & Baker's profit growth for the first half of 2003 (January-June, 2003) was 88%.

-    NEIMETH International Pharmaceuticals Plc   recorded 105% increase in its profit before tax in its financial year ended March 31, 2003. (Nigerian Tribune, 17th September 2003).

-    NAFDAC activities have reinforced the   confidence of investors in the pharmaceutical industry, as evidenced in the continuous upward movement in the share prices of the pharmaceutical companies quoted in the Nigerian stock exchange.

-    The Agency's reforms have led to renewed confidence

and increased patronage of drugs produced in Nigeria by other West African countries. This has resulted in the lifting of ban on made in Nigeria drugs by some West African countries.

-   Many Multinational Drug Companies are coming back to Nigeria due to improved regulatory environment.

-   From April 2001 to June 2004; the Agency has carried out seventy-six destruction exercises of counterfeit and substandard products valued at almost N7.2 billion (US$50 million). Over 1100 containers of regulated products were placed on 'Hold' at the Port Harcourt and Lagos ports, and most of the owners have absconded. In 2002, a total of 209 raids were carried out on distribution outlets of counterfeit drugs while 280 raids were conducted from January – September, 2003.

-   Presently, we have secured 30 convictions in respect of counterfeit drugs related cases. In such convictions, the courts have always ordered the forfeiture of the violative products to the Federal Government for destruction. Over forty cases against violators are still pending in various courts.

-   Even though we have not concluded the second phase of our baseline study, current reports have revealed that the incidence of unregistered drugs has drastically reduced by about 80%. Our target is to reduce to the barest minimum the incidence of counterfeit drugs in Nigeria by the end of 2004.

-   NAFDAC monitors salt iodization in Nigeria and in this regard, UNICEF rated Nigeria as the first country in Africa to achieve universal salt iodization. We have 100% compliance at Manufacturers and Distributors levels and 98% at household level. The success on salt iodization was made possible by UNICEF who supplied us testing kits and trained our staff on how to use them.

\-   There are cheering reports of declining number of kidney failure patients and death rates in our hospitals. We are working in concert with all Government hospitals in Nigeria, by compiling the number of renal patients and deaths on monthly basis in order to establish a trend.

\-   Immense public awareness created by NAFDAC on its regulatory activities, especially on fake/ counterfeit drugs resulted in the participation of the regulated industries, consumers and other stakeholders in the promotion of food and drug regulation in Nigeria. These achievements among many others have awakened the international consciousness that Nigeria is no longer a dumping ground for fake drugs."

Almost all the highlighted achievements and gains as presented by the chief executive of NAFDAC are fully supported by the data, exhibits, tables of activities by the Narcotics & Control Substances Directorate, Breakdown of Samples Analysed between April 2001 and 2004, Summary of Foreign GMP Inspections conducted in year 2001 to 2004. on cosmetics, medical devices, food and drugs. The table by Registration & Regulatory Affairs Directorate showing the upsurge in number of completed application forms received and number of registered regulated products are quite convincing, especially the graphical illustration showing the steadily growing trends. All the above have proved that the chief executive has very high level of integrity and have therefore provided adequate answers to the research question 2 and have proved hypothesis no. 2 to be correct.

Further Analysis of the data for Answers to Research question 3

The research question 3 is restated: Is there any evidence of increase in productivity and improved performance in the investigated organization under the leadership of the current chief executive? The corresponding hypothesis (Hypothesis 3) also restated: The increase in productivity and the improved performance in the investigated organization is due to the leadership ability of the current chief executive.

The above interview data as well as the secondary data are full of evidence of increase in productivity and improved performance in NAFDAC under the leadership of the current chief executive. The chief executive of NAFDAC during the interview reported that when her new management came on board, the appalling state of the organization was an emergency that demanded attention. She reportedly transformed the pressure into positive drive to turn around the system for better. She went further to say that the rebirth was made possible through hard work, honesty, transparency and unalloyed commitment of the staff. In addition to the rebirth, she cited 13 achievements reproduced under section 5.2.3., that could easily be verified using the various tables under appendix 4. The increase in productivity and improved performance under the leadership of the NAFDAC current chief executive are very outstanding that various stakeholders acknowledged these openly and went ahead to give various local and international awards and honours to the chief executive. Some of these are presented as exhibits under appendix 4. All these are verifiable evidence, and it can therefore be said that there are increases in productivity and improved performance under the leadership of the chief executive of NAFDAC.

Further analysis of the data for Answers to Research Question 4

The research question 4 is restated: Is there any evidence that the increase in productivity and improved performance of the organization has something to do with the integrity of the chief executive? The corresponding hypothesis (Hypothesis 4) states: A chief executive that has integrity will positively influence increase in productivity and improved performance in an organization. Again it could be said that there are so many evidence that will provide positive answers to this research question. It has already been proved that the chief executive has high level of integrity. The situation on ground before her assumption of office in April, 2001, was appalling and demanded immediate attention because corruption had rendered the regulatory activity of the agency very ineffective for over two decades and the whole economic environment was nearly grounded totally with the attendant risky health situation all over the country. However, according to the chief executive of NAFDAC, on resumption as the chief executive she instituted the culture that promoted transparency, accountability and abhors corruption. She cited this as the greatest of the achievement and gains in NAFDAC under her. During the interview with her, she also stated that she had to terminate the appointment of her brother-in-law who was caught in act of corruption, because she has a duty to lead by example Besides these points, the stakeholders and other players in the economy acknowledged that the positive changes in NAFDAC were all as a result of the positive influence of the chief executive. This is in agreement with the argument of Bryman (1992) who defined leadership in terms of social influence. In some of the exhibits under appendix 4, the chief executive of NAFDAC was given national and international awards for her determined fight against corruption and fake drugs barons at the risk of her life. She had survived about two assassination attempts on her life as a result of the fight against corruption and against fake drug pushers.

All the above accounts are strong evidence to support the positive answers to question 4. There are positive confirmation that there are increases in productivity and improved performance in the organization under her leadership. These increases in productivity and improved performance have a lot to do with the integrity of the chief executive because such increase in productivity and improved performance did not occur for over two decades until she resumed as the chief executive on the 12th of April, 2001, with determination to succeed through hard work, honesty, and transparency. The numerous evidence cited above proved that she influenced the attitudinal change of staff and other stakeholders, for example the attitude of staff to bribery changed and they now struggled to gain rapid promotion through catching big company involved in importing expired products and other unhealthy materials. The woman who caught Nestle, for example was promoted to Director level. She made this very clear during the interview and also in her paper presentation. As she was quoted above, the revival of NAFDAC activities and the rebirth could not have happened without attitudinal change of staff and stakeholders. She stated clearly that in transforming NAFDAC, corruption and conflict of interest were amongst the major challenges faced. According to her, corruption is a driving force for poor regulation, which encourages drug faking/counterfeiting. She however, reported that all the ugly practices have been drastically reduced to pave way for fake drug eradication and creation of a strong regulatory environment. In other words she fought and reduced corruption drastically and the attitudes of the staff of NAFDAC were changed for good.

Further Analysis of the Data for Answers to Research Question 5

Question 5 restated: Is the suggestion of trait theory that organizations will work better if people in managerial positions have designated leadership profiles valid and applicable in these organizations under investigation?

Hypothesis 5: Organizations in Nigeria will work better and achieve good results if people in leadership positions have integrity.

In the final conclusion of her paper presented at the Lagos Business School Breakfast Club Meeting, on 6th July, 2004, she stated:

"The success recorded by NAFDAC show that excellent performance in the public sector is possible with the right spirit and right team. Bureaucratic bottlenecks and all forms of corruption that are the bane of the public sector can be overcome to improve performance. If one person ignites the flame for good leadership in Nigeria and passes the touch to other people in a manner that they can identify with, the entire country shall surely be lit up. I therefore encourage CEOs and other heads of Public and Private Sector Organizations to ignite these flames in their various organizations and let the country glow with good leadership."

The above statements could not have come from a corrupt and ineffective leader. These are statements expected from exemplary leaders with high level of integrity. It could therefore be said at this stage that there should be little or no doubt that the chief executive of NAFDAC possesses integrity and that this was mainly responsible for her outstanding success in an organization that had experienced failure and poor performance for more than two decades before she became the chief executive. This has been acknowledged openly all over the world and in Nigeria as well and could be seen as additional evidence to support the argument that she has integrity. For example, in 2003, the Transparency International (TI) gave her Integrity Award along with former Auditor General of Samoa, and Anna Hazare, an Indian campaigner against corruption in forestry and in government. Professor Akunyili has earned nationwide respect for her persistence in prosecuting illegal drug traders despite several death threats. The Transparency International Integrity award was given on the 25th of May, 2003, during the 11th International Anti-Corruption Conference (IACC) in Seoul, Korea, and hosted by the government of South Korea (see exhibit 1 and 2, under appendix 4 for details).

Apart from this she has also received many other awards including the EMRC award from the Belgian European Marketing Research Centre in 2005, in recognition of the "highly professional way and seriousness" with which the NAFDAC Boss has treated the quality of processed food in Nigeria for the past four years. The Belgian Ambassador to Nigeria has also described the work of NAFDAC as an important economic intervention and image-making support by the Federal Government. In addition to these, she was also conferred with the 2004 Economic Crime Fighters Award by United Kingdom based ICC Commercial Crime Services Bureau, and in 2005 she was named the sole recipient of the 2005 Grassroot Human Rights Campaigner Award by the London based Human Rights Defense organization (see details in exhibit 4, under appendix 4). The BBC Documentary showing the relentless battle being waged against fake drugs in Nigeria by Professor Dora Akunyili's led NAFDAC, won the prestigious Pulitzer Prize for television in June, 2006.

A visiting French Minister, Mrs Christine Lagarde , described the NAFDAC boss as a "shinning model and international star" worthy of emulation by men and women in public service. She praised Akunyili for her valour and courage in daring to wage a vigorous battle against fake drug barons even in the face of threats to her life. The Time Magazine Award was also given to her as "one of the 18 heroes of our time", and this was openly acknowledged by the President of the Federal Republic of Nigeria, who admitted that the Time Magazine did not make a mistake in selecting her as one of the heroes of our time. The

President observed that the NAFDAC boss was one figure whose contributions to national development had been outstanding in recent times. He pointed out that she had implemented the NAFDAC Policy beyond the expectations of the Federal Government, particularly her relentless war against the marketing of fake and substandard drugs and consumables. He added that for a woman, who had stuck out her neck in order that others might live, it did not come to him as a surprise that Time Magazine recognized her (for the details see exhibits 5, and 6, under appendix 4).

All these are additional facts and evidence to support the argument about the possession of integrity by a leader and the great effects this can have on the followers and the productivity and growth of the organization. It could rightly be said that the increase in productivity and the improved performance in NAFDAC is due mainly to the leadership ability of the chief executive. It is therefore correct to say that a chief executive that has integrity will positively influence increase in productivity and improved performance in an organization. Dora Akunyili, the chief executive of NAFDAC has reasonably proved both in her leadership qualities and the results she achieved in the organization, that the trait approach to leadership (Northouse, 2001) is applicable in NAFDAC and therefore in Nigeria. The suggestion of trait theory that organizations will work better if people in managerial positions have designated leadership profiles is valid and applicable in NAFDAC. It could therefore be said that organizations in Nigeria will work better and achieve good results if people in leadership position have integrity (Hypothesis 5).

CHAPTER SIX

*DATA PRESENTATION, EVALUATION
AND ANALYSIS ON NEIMETH
UNDER MAZI SAM OHUABUNWA*

Introduction

This chapter is also devoted for presentation of report, interview data, evaluation, analysis and discussion of the outcome of the interview conducted with the chief executive of Neimeth International Pharmaceuticals Plc. The aim again is to present how a leader has provided leadership that brought trust and commitment in the organization and made things happen. The summary report of the facts gathered about the organization and the interview with the chief executive have therefore been presented and discussed in this chapter.

Brief Historical Background

According to the company's profile, Neimeth International Pharmaceuticals Plc is the resultant company from the Mazi Sam I. Ohuabunwa (chief executive) led Management-Buy-Out of the 60% equity holding of Pfizer Inc, New York, USA, in Pfizer Products Plc (Nigeria). This Management-Buy-Out according to the chief executive took place in May 1997 (during the difficult period of military rule of the late General Abacha) when Pfizer Inc, in pursuit of its global repositioning strategy, divested 60% equity in Pfizer Products Plc, in favour of the existing management.

The name Neimeth, according to the chief executive, was chosen to honour Mr. Robert Neimeth, an American who contributed immensely to the establishment of Pfizer in Nigeria. According to the report, Mr. Neimeth relentlessly used his position to stop Pfizer's early divestment from Nigeria as a result of his belief in the economic potentials of Nigeria and its strategic importance in Africa. The company's profile had it that Neimeth could rightly be said to be the "alien father" of Pfizer operations in Nigeria, especially as a manufacturer. The chief executive of Neimeth International Pharmaceuticals Plc, Mazi Ohuabunwa confirmed that Mr Neimeth during his time in Nigeria was very much in support of Nigeria because of her great economic potentials and the people's enterprise. According to him, Neimeth then, observed that the only problem with Nigeria was leadership, and that Nigeria would become a great nation as soon as she overcomes the leadership problem. Mr Neimeth retired as President, Pfizer International Pharmaceuticals Group in January 1997, and in May of the same year, Pfizer Inc, divested its shares in Pfizer Products Plc.

According to the account, prior to this divestment and subsequent change of name to Neimeth, the company had operated in Nigeria for 40 years, manufacturing, marketing, and distributing Pfizer brands of pharmaceutical and veterinary products in tablets, capsules, ointment/cream, powder, injectables, and oral liquid forms. During the 40 year period (1957 to 1997), the company established the first pharmaceutical manufacturing plant in Nigeria at Aba, which was destroyed during the Nigerian civil war. It then set up and opened the most modern pharmaceutical plant in the West African sub-region in 1976 at Oregun, Lagos. These represent great milestones for a company that started as a trading venture in 1957 at a location in Ebute Metta, Lagos.

Neimeth Metamorphosis, New Opportunities, And New Challenges.

According to the profile, at inception, Neimeth business operation was anchored on its manufacturing and distribution licence agreements with Pfizer. The manufacturing licence allowed Neimeth to manufacture, market and distribute Pfizer's traditional brands in Nigeria while the distribution agreement allowed Neimeth to distribute the newer, high-tech Pfizer brands imported as finished products. According to the report, this co-operation with Pfizer has remained in place and was recently strengthened when Pfizer allowed Neimeth to sell TCP in the West African market. Also following these agreements, Neimeth benefits from Pfizer technical supervision to ensure maintenance of Good Manufacturing Practice (GMP) standards to international levels.

With the divestment, however, Neimeth now enjoys the flexibility to develop new alliances with other international companies to increase its product portfolio, establish new business opportunities, as well as develop its own brand of generic products to meet local healthcare needs. According to the chief executive, Neimeth is also at liberty to develop her own new products from natural or synthetic moieties for the enhancement of healthcare delivery needs. This entails collaboration with local researchers in specific disease areas. The chief executive said that enormous opportunities and potentials are now open to Neimeth for business expansion and growth. He added that the company is now better placed to meet her new vision/mission having shed the compulsion to align with Pfizer's global vision, which does not necessarily take cognizance of key disease areas in the organization's developing world or environment.

Neimeth International Pharmaceuticals Plc Strategic Policy Change

The new opportunities and challenges according to the profile, necessitated a constructive development of inwardly looking corporate operational policies and guidelines that best meet the needs and aspirations of Neimeth's healthcare and challenges. The organization's new policy direction is:

-       To seek business alliances with reputable international pharmaceutical companies with the objective of selectively introducing their useful products into the Nigerian /ECOWAS market;

-       To go into collaborative agreements with local researchers with a view to developing "home grown" drugs for specific ailments in key disease areas that plague our people (It is important to point out that under the current leadership, Neimeth had already achieved a breakthrough with their flagship home grown product, CIKLAVIT for the management of sickle cell disease within this short period);

-       To deliberately foray into the manufacturing of affordable branded generics in common disease areas for use of our primary healthcare system.

-       To deliberately encourage, facilitate, and partake in public awareness/advocacy programmes aimed at preventing or eradicating common preventable diseases.

Neimeth Stated Corporate Ideology, Shared Values and Guiding Philosophy:

-       **NEIMETH VISION**

Neimeth vision is to be the leading pharmaceutical company and a leader in corporate Nigeria, through the achievement of excellence in delivering competitive and high quality products and services.

- NEIMETH MISSION

Neimeth performance will be driven by the resolve to be the Number 1 pharmaceutical company in Nigeria, maintaining enviable employee welfare scheme and through the provision of quality products and superior returns to all stakeholders while adding value to indigenous research.

- TEAM WORK

Neimeth expects staff to approach their tasks with the spirit of teamwork, sharing responsibilities and rewards with each other, in an environment of trust and friendship.

- LEADERSHIP

In Neimeth there is commitment to provide the opportunity for leadership at all levels in the organization, the pharmaceutical industry and indeed the Nation.

- INNOVATION

Neimeth leadership believes that by doing things differently, building a foundation on new and proven ideas, they can change any market situation. Their commitment to innovation means they will continuously introduce better and efficacious products to meet changing market needs.

- CUSTOMER FOCUS

Neimeth leadership believes that their customers are the bedrock of their market position. They are committed to meeting the needs of their customers and satisfying their desires by striving to offer them the best quality products at the best prices always.

- INTEGRITY

At Neimeth the leadership expects their stakeholders to possess integrity and they demand same of themselves. Openness, honesty, and ethical conduct must characterize their transactions.

- PERFORMANCE

The leadership of Neimeth believes that the organization's performance will earn them the respect that they deserve in the industry and communities of interest, and so they set high performance standards for themselves and business associates.

- COMMUNITY

As a corporate citizen Neimeth gives her best to the communities in which it operates. By improving the well being of these communities, the organization receives commensurate rewards from them because the corporate life is tied to the organization's well-being.

- RESPONSIVENESS

The leadership of Neimeth believes that their corporate success is based on the excellence of their people. They strive to be responsive to their employees, customers and the general public by encouraging free flow of information.

- GOD CONSCIOUSNESS

The leadership of Neimeth believes that the Almighty God created Heaven and the Earth and all that are within them. They recognize the sovereign character of God and His love for mankind. Their desire is to do God's will and in all their dealings to reflect their love and respect for Him, knowing full well that they need divine guidance to successfully and consistently accomplish their mission/vision.

Introduction – Your organization has been perceived as a successful one that merit closer assessment for research purpose. What is your own assessment of this organization that you have managed for more than four years? What is the origin of Neimeth and how is the organization doing today?

First Response – In response to the above introductory questions, the chief executive said that Neimeth International Pharmaceuticals Plc is the resultant company from the Mazi Sam I. Ohuabunwa led Management-Buy-Out of the 60% equity holding of Pfizer Inc., New York, USA, in Pfizer Products Plc., Nigeria. According to him this Management-Buy-Out took place in May 1997 when Pfizer Inc. in pursuit of its global repositioning strategy decided to divest her 60% equity in Pfizer Products Plc, in favour of the existing management and to pull out of Nigeria during the very difficult economic environment under late General Sani Abacha. Prior to this divestment and subsequent change of name to Neimeth, Pfizer had operated in Nigeria for 40 years, manufacturing, marketing, and distributing Pfizer brands of pharmaceutical and veterinary products in tablets, capsules, ointment/cream, powder, injectables, and oral liquid forms. The chief executive further said that during the 40 year period (1957-1997), Pfizer established the first pharmaceutical manufacturing plant in Nigeria at Aba, which was destroyed during the Nigerian civil war. The organization then set up and opened the most modern pharmaceutical plant in the West African sub-region in 1976 at Oregun, Lagos.

According to the chief executive, before the name of the new company was selected, several names were considered but on

Easter Monday, 1997, the name Neimeth flashed through and was immediately chosen to honour Mr Robert Neimeth, an American who contributed immensely to the establishment of Pfizer in Nigeria, and was a very good friend of Nigeria during his time as the Managing Director of Pfizer. He said that Mr Neimeth relentlessly used his position to stop Pfizer's early divestment from Nigeria as a result of his belief in the economic potentials of Nigeria and its strategic importance in Africa. This name was not approved initially as the departing executives of Pfizer Inc was not sure that Mr Neimeth would accept it and therefore insisted that Mr Neimeth's approval for the use of his name must be sought and obtained first. According to Mazi Sam Ohuabunwa, his group wrote and obtained the approval of Mr Neimeth who not only gave his approval for his name to be used but also felt honoured by the gesture and was in Nigeria in person for the inauguration. According to the chief executive, Mr Robert Neimeth could be said to be the "alien father" of Pfizer operations in Nigeria, especially as a manufacturer. He confirmed that Mr Neimeth retired as President, Pfizer International Pharmaceuticals Groups in January, 1997, and in May the same year, Pfizer Inc. divested its shares in Pfizer Products Plc., Nigeria.

The chief executive of Neimeth International Pharmaceuticals Plc stated that Neimeth as an organization has a unique passion for excellence, passion for professionalism and superior services. He said that they were committed to their unwavering desire to delight the stakeholders, to deliver on their promises and to be ethical in the conduct of their business. He added that following the successes recorded at the "first most successful" Management Buy-Out in Nigeria, Neimeth has become a reference point in innovative and strategic financial management, stakeholders intimacy and social responsiveness, which have contributed to Neimeth reputation as a reliable, credible and trustworthy company. He said that with this status, comes an even greater commitment to meeting the ever-growing health-care needs of Nigeria and the West African Sub-Region. He said that the resolve of the management of Neimeth is to be the No. 1 Pharmaceutical Company in Nigeria, consistently improving profitability while maintaining an enviable employee welfare scheme, through the provision of quality products and adding of superior returns to all shareholders.

The chief executive of Neimeth International Pharmaceutical Plc, Mazi Sam Ohuabunwa was at this point asked: "Has integrity anything to do with the outstanding success of the organization?" Response: "It has, because whatever a man sows he reaps". He talk about honesty and went further to elaborate by saying: "In Pfizer, the company subscribes to core values and have entrenched integrity and the fear of God into the system, and expects the staff to demonstrate these values. Before any one is picked up for higher responsibility the management would first look for integrity and industry". He cited the example of what happened before he was appointed a Regional Manager, West Africa, Pfizer in 1993. He said that unknown to him, the visitor from the Pfizer head office had gone around to gather comments and reports on him from the local observers and stakeholders. This was a demonstration of how serious the company took the issue of integrity and the relevant qualities. According to him, appointment to a leadership position demands integrity of the officer and must be confirmed by relevant stakeholders. He went further to say that the organization's core values based on integrity and the fear of God expect that employees should: "Try to be the best of what you are; Seek the best for the stakeholders and desire to be fair and seek to protect their interest; Those around who interact must see these values in the officer." He said that this has led Neimeth into privileges and helped to open doors for the organization. For example, according to him the loan the new management obtained for the management buy-out of the 60% equity of the Pfizer Inc., was obtained because of trust. He said: "When the last cheque for the loan was written, the company received commendation from the bank's chairman". He said that: "Banks look for integrity before parting with their money". The chief executive of Neimeth believes that integrity opens business opportunity because the company is seen as organization that has men and women of integrity who keep their words.

The chief executive in response to the question on his No.1 strength that he could recommend to any leader who wants to succeed like him, said: "Yes integrity based on the fear of God is No.1. I know that God rewards, so equity and fairness take upper hand." "In Neimeth, our pricing strategy is costs plus marginal mark-up. Even if the products become scarce in the market, we do not take undue advantage by increasing the price, but allow the existing price to remain irrespective of the temporary gains such increase in price might bring to the company. Pleasing God drives our relationship with customers. In our organization we have vision to be a company of integrity with ethical values, we are working to get to a higher height, and we are yet to get there. Leading with integrity has helped me as a leader to maintain good relationship with my subordinates and the employees generally. I do receive encouraging letters of commendation from subordinates and other employees and employer with such statements as 'we believe in you and you did not let us down'." "It is the integrity that drives me." "I lead by example, if I say that subordinates should work for 12 hours I would make sure that I work 13 hours."

The chief executive was at this point asked to state other specific lessons he would want Nigerian leaders and others to learn from his experience for successful leadership. He responded by saying that: "Best leaders are those who have their inert skills, and have continued to top it up with additional knowledge from time to time." He said that continuous self- development is very important.

He was then asked to express his views based on his experience, on the argument that leaders are born and not made. He responded by saying: "Some are born and some are made. There are those who have the natural propensity, and I have watched leaders emerge naturally and I enjoy them. They take initiative. There is also a place for acquiring leadership skills, and a person that has intrinsic values can develop it further and this makes you outstanding." He recounted that he had the leadership urge even at the secondary school days when he became the president of many societies while a secondary school student. He stated that this continued at various stages in his life.

Furthermore, the chief executive of Neimeth International Pharmaceuticals Plc was asked to confirm if the NAFDAC (National Agency for Food and Drug Administration and Control) activities had any effects on his organization Neimeth, and his leadership. He responded by saying that: "The NAFDAC activities have positive impacts on the pharmaceutical industry as a whole. In the late 90s the fortunes of the industry declined as a result of unfair competitions brought about by dumping of foreign cheap and fake products from abroad. It was bad for the industry from 1998 to 2000. However, since NAFDAC under the leadership of Professor Akunyili came and began to confront the problems and created awareness of the existence of fake drugs and effectively blocked the flow, there has been up turn and the situation has changed. Today a number of people are setting up new plants in the pharmaceutical industry. NAFDAC played a positive role in this".

He was finally asked if he had any vision for Neimeth for the next five years. He started to answer this question by saying that: "Every leader needs some kind of assessment otherwise the leader becomes a victim of mob praise. The leader should be subjected to new information and ideas always, ever knowing that the day you stop you can become obsolete. Every leader must have core value. There must be something you anchor on so that when the wind blows you can still stand. There must be a vision for effective leadership. The leader must be focused. He or she may stop half way, but this makes him/her work straight, and the followers will know where the leader is going. Vision causes the level of activities and the resources needed to be realized. The philosophical base is necessary. Leaders must have a way of assessing their performance. Whatever you do not measure will not have a good standard."

For the five years vision for Neimeth, the chief executive has this to say: "I believe that Neimeth will be amongst the top three leading pharmaceuticals company in Nigeria. It will be the leading research-based company in Nigeria."

The interview was brought to an end at this point and the researcher expressed appreciation to the chief executive for all the co-operation and useful contributions to this important study. The chief executive was delighted and further volunteered more information by way of published reports and annual financial statements. Some of the financial statements and annual performance reports are reproduced below for easy reference and analysis.

Table 6.1. NEIMETH INTERNATIONAL FIVE YEAR FINANCIAL SUMMARY

	2005	2004	2003	2002	2001
ASSETS	**N'000**	**N'000**	**N'000**	**N'000**	**N'000**
Fixed Assets	72,221	54,800	59,352	76,010	96,389
Net Current Assets	938,002	896,653	294,903	231,300	169,431
Prov.for liabilities& charges	(469,304)	(532,459)	(45,794)	(46,219)	(32,489)
Total	**540,919**	**418,994**	**308,461**	**261,091**	**233,331**
CAPITAL & RESERVES					
Share Capital	92,524	82,103	69,538	56,867	56,517
Share premium account	236,408	204,826	141,402	130,725	127,603
General reserve	193,482	132,065	97,521	62,126	49,211
Reserve for bonus issue	18,505	-	-	11,373	-
Shareholders funds	**540,919**	**418,994**	**308,461**	**261,091**	**233,331**
TURNOVER	1,241,949	1,002,024	950,804	897,811	1,003,036
Profit/Loss before taxation	153,602	89,155	72,386	35,215	30,043
Profit/Loss after taxation	98,427	59,175	52,084	35,661	21,057
Dividend	37,010	24,631	16,689	11,373	-
Earnings per 50K share	53	36	37	26	15
Dividend per 50K share	20	15	10	8	-

Source: Neimeth International's Published Annual Reports and
Financial Statements.

Table 6.2. PROFIT AND LOSS ACCOUNT FOR THE YEAR ENDED 31 ST MARCH, 2005

	2005	2004
	N'000	N'000
INCOME		
Turnover	1,241,949	1,002,024
Cost of Sales	(478,331)	(364,490)
Gross Profit	763,618	637,534
Profit on disposal of fixed assets	533	380
Other Income	140	6,503
	764,291	**644,417**
DEDUCT: EXPENSES		
Marketing and distribution expenses	228,509	189,305
Administrative expenses	193,295	170,342
Finance charges	161,998	170,993
Bad debts written off	633	1,622
Provision for doubtful account	26,254	23,000
	610,689	**555,262**
Profit before taxation	153,602	89,155
Taxation	(55,175)	(29,980)
Profit for the year after taxation	**98,427**	**59,175**
Proposed dividend	(37,010)	(24,631)
Retained profit transferred to general reserve	**61,417**	**34,544**
Earnings per share (Kobo)	53	36
Dividend per share (Kobo)	20	15

Source: Neimeth International's published annual financial statements

Table 6.3. NEIMETH INTERNATIONAL BALANCE SHEET AS AT 31 ST MARCH, 2005

	2005	2004
	N'000	N'000
FIXED ASSETS	**72,221**	**54,800**
CURRENT ASSETS		
Stock	865,029	780,681
Debtors and prepayments	507,597	449,907
Forex purchased for import	89,538	151,549
Cash and bank balances	92,936	79,248
	1,555,100	**1,461,385**
CREDITORS: Amounts falling due within 12 months	(617,098)	(564,732)
Net current assets	**938,002**	**896,653**
Total assets less current liabilities	**1,010,223**	**951,453**
CREDITORS: Amount falling due after more than one year		
Debenture stock	(384,093)	(480,093)
PROVISION FOR LIABILITIES AND CHARGES		
Deferred taxation	(15,002)	(13,881)
Provision for gratuity	(70,209)	(38,485)
	540,919	**418,994**
CAPITAL AND RESERVES		
Share capital	92,524	82,103
Share premium	236,408	204,826
Revenue reserve	193,482	132,065
Reserve for bonus issue	18,505	-
SHAREHOLDERS FUNDS	**540,919**	**418,994**

SOURCE: Neimeth International's published annual financial statement.

Analysis And Discussion Of Data

This section is devoted to the analysis and discussion of data collected through the perceived leader integrity scale (PLIS) of Craig and Gustafson (1998), the questionnaires, interviews, and secondary data, all relating to the studies carried out in the Neimeth International Pharmaceuticals Plc as explained above. All these analyses are geared towards answering all the research questions and proving the hypotheses that are all focused on leadership with integrity. The effective analysis of these data and satisfactory answers to all the research questions will help us to advance the argument and relate specific trait like integrity to the leadership outcome like productivity or growth of the organization. Ultimately it will be possible to see the effects of these analysed data on the trait theory which suggests that an organization will work better if the people in managerial positions have designated leadership profiles, especially from the Nigerian context. The summary of the findings are presented as the data analysis progresses. The discussions and analysis relate to the findings in the Neimeth International Pharmaceuticals Plc as earlier stated.

The first relevant research question here is Research Question 1 – Can the integrity of the chief executive of the organization be confirmed by the immediate subordinates in the same organization? The corresponding hypothesis is Hypothesis 1 – The immediate subordinates of a chief executive that has integrity, will notice it, feel the impact of it, and can testify to it. The other relevant questions under this are research questions 2 and 4, and the corresponding hypothesis are hypothesis 2 and 4.

The Perceived Leadership Integrity Scale (PLIS) of Craig and Gustafson (1998) is used here to find answer to the research question 1 and others. In answering research question 1, using the above standard and format (PLIS), the questionnaires that were completed by the immediate subordinates to the chief executive at Neimeth International Pharmaceuticals Plc, were summarized and analysed as shown below in table 6.4., for the answer to research question 1.

Table 6.4: Summary Scores of PLIS in Neimeth International

Subordinates	1	2	3	4	Total	Average
Scores	31	31	36	37	**135**	**33.75**

Out of five immediate subordinates that were given the questionnaires for completion, four completed and returned theirs, and this gives 80% returns. Two out of the four scored the chief executive 31. The two scores mean that the chief executive is rated highly ethical, which means that he has high level of integrity. The third subordinate scored him 36 and the fourth scored him 37. These two scores were within the range of 36 –

66, which stands for moderate. Altogether the scores of the four subordinates are found to be within the range of 31 – 37. When the scores were summed up individually, the average was found to be 33.75. It could therefore be said that the average scores given by the subordinates fall within the range of 31 - 35 and this is the range that stands for high ethical. From these scores the chief executive of Neimeth International Pharmaceuticals Plc could be said to have been rated high ethical by his subordinates. In other words he has high level of integrity going by the assessment of his immediate subordinates. It could also be said that hypothesis 1 has been proved correct in Neimeth International Pharmaceuticals Plc. This is to say that the immediate subordinates of the chief executive of Neimeth have observed and felt the impact of the genuine integrity of their boss and have also testified to it. Based on all these facts it could be confirmed that the chief executive of Neimeth is also a leader with integrity.

Further Data Analysis for Answers to Research Questions 2

In this section, further analysis and answers to research questions 2 are provided, using interview data and secondary data as well as the PLIS as they relate to Neimeth International Pharmaceuticals Plc. The research question 2 is therefore restated: Is there any evidence that the chief executive of the successful organization under investigation has high level of integrity? The corresponding hypothesis (Hypothesis 2) states: The success of the organization and the confirmation of the immediate subordinates will show that the chief executive of the investigated successful organization has high level of integrity.

The analysis already done, has provided answers for research question 2 already. The immediate subordinates in Neimeth International Pharmaceuticals Plc, averagely scored their chief executive very high on integrity. The four immediate subordinates in Neimeth International Pharmaceuticals Plc gave average score of 33.75, which also falls within the range of 31 – 35 (high ethical). This stands for high level of integrity, and so it can logically be said that there is evidence that the chief executive in the successful organization investigated (Neimeth International Pharmaceuticals Plc) has high level of integrity. Further analysis and answering of the questions were carried out below, using the interview data and the secondary data obtained from Neimeth International Pharmaceuticals Plc.

Neimeth Interview Data Analysis

Using the same approach, the interview data obtained from the Neimeth chief executive was analysed, and it was found also that some of the responses and statements on some of the interview questions were quite revealing and convincing and could also provide answers to research questions 2. For example, during the interview with the chief executive of Neimeth International Pharmaceuticals Plc, Mazi Sam Ohuabunwa, he was asked to explain what he did to earn the subordinates' and staff trust and commitment to the goals of the organization. He was specifically asked to explain if integrity has anything to do with the outstanding successes. In his response he said:

"It has, because whatever a man sows he reaps. Our former organization, Pfizer, established a system that promotes honesty and before anyone is picked for higher responsibility in the organization, the leadership must consider two key core values – integrity and industry."

He went further to elaborate on the above by narrating his experience in the former organization, Pfizer, when he was to be promoted as a Regional Manager, West Africa.

He said that before his promotion, there was a visitor from their head office, whose mission was to quietly and privately assess his reliability and integrity through the local stakeholders who have been dealing with him at the local level. The organization believes that the local stakeholders are in a good position to observe and report the activities of the potential candidate. He went further to say that based on the above background the company has entrenched couple of values as follow:

"Our company subscribes to core values – integrity is cherished, and the fear of God. Our staff are encouraged to try to be the best of what they are, to seek the best for the stakeholders, desire to be fair and seek to protect the interests of the stakeholders. Those who interact with us must see the values."

"This has led Neimeth into privileges and opened doors for the company. The chairman of the bank that gave the loan, said: "Sam I trust you". When the last cheque was written the company received commendation from the bank. Banks look for integrity, and I believe that it opens business opportunity because our company is seen as company of men of integrity – men who keep their words."

The above responses and statements are quite clear and when content analysis is done on these it becomes clear and easy to notice that integrity and issues that relates to integrity and its values and benefits dominates the responses and statements.

During the interview, the chief executive was also asked to state his No. 1 strength that he could recommend to any leader who wants to succeed like him. He responded as follow:

"I know that God rewards, so equity and fairness take upper hand – integrity based on the fear of God is No.1. In pricing for example we do costs plus minimal margin to get minimum pricing level. If products become scarce we do not take undue advantage to increase the price, we maintain the same price level. In our company we do not yet possess the level we wish but we have vision to be a

company of integrity with high ethical values."

"Integrity has helped me – I receive encouraging letters of commendation from employer and employees telling me that they believe in me and that I did not let them down. It is integrity that drives me. I try to lead by example – if I say that staff should work for 12 hours I must make sure I work for 13 hours."

The thorough analysis of all the above responses and statements portrays the chief executive of Neimeth to be of high level of integrity. It is not only from the point of view of the immediate subordinates as has been confirmed earlier, using the PLIS. The employer is also confirming it. The operating standard of the organization is also another source. It could therefore be said that integrity of the leader is very instrumental to the improved performance of the organization and the increase in productivity.

Further Data Analysis for Answers to Research Question 3

The research question 3 is restated: Is there any evidence of increase in productivity and improved performance in the investigated organization under the leadership of the current chief executive? The corresponding hypothesis (Hypothesis 3) states: The increase in productivity and the improved performance in the investigated organization is due to the leadership ability of the current chief executive. The research question 3 is raised to find out if there is any evidence of increase in productivity and improved performance in the investigated organization under the leadership of the current chief executive. The interview data and the secondary data already presented above provide adequate evidence and answers to this research question. For example, tables 6.1, 6.2, and 6.3 presented above readily reveal that Neimeth International Pharmaceuticals Plc, for five years from 2001 to 2005 had maintained continuous increase in turnover, profits, shareholders' funds, capital, dividends and earnings per share.

For example the shareholders fund reached 233,331,000 Naira in 2001. It increased by 12% in 2002, and increased further by 18% in 2003. As a result of continuous improved performance the shareholders fund rose again by 35% in 2004 and there was a further increase of 29% in 2005 that pushed the shareholders fund to 540,919,000 Naira by the end of the year. Apart from the steady growth of shareholders funds, the five-year financial summary in table 6.1. above also showed that the profit after tax had also grown steadily from 2001 to 2005. This grew by 69.4%, from 21,057,000 Naira in 2001 to 35,661,000 Naira in 2002, and by 46% in 2003, to the figure of 52,084,000 Naira. It grew again by 13.6% in 2004 and grew at a very high rate of 63% in 2005, to the figure of 98,427,000 Naira.

The same table 6.1., shows that the dividend declared by the organization also witnessed steady increase in rate from 2001 to 2005. The rate increased in 2003 by 46.7% when compared with the dividend declared in 2002. In 2004 this increased again by 47.6% when compared with the dividend of 2003. In 2005 it increased by 50.3% when compared with the figure of 2004. The total turnover of the organization as shown in the same table 6.1., had also witnessed steady growth from 897,811,000 Naira in 2002 to 950,804,000 Naira in 2003, and to 1,002,024,000 Naira in 2004, and subsequently to 1,241,949,000 in 2005. Table 6.2., showing the profit and loss account for the year ended 31st March, 2005 also revealed a healthy growth of turnover, gross profit, and earnings per share when compared with that of 2004. The balance sheet items like assets, share capital, share premium and revenue reserve also showed healthy growth when compared with the figures of 2004 as revealed in the organization's balance sheet as at 31st March, 2005 reproduced as table 6.3.

Apart from all these the organization was also able to launch a new product known as Ciklavit for the management of sickle cell disease, and this was proudly presented as Nigerian product at the WHO (World Health Organization) Summit in September, 2006. In addition to these, the loan with which the 60% equity of the Pfizer Inc was purchased in 1997 was fully paid off within a short period as stated by the chief executive during the interview. All these increases and achievements could not have been possible without increase in productivity and improved performance. From the outcome of this investigation it could be concluded that all these are strong evidence that the organization has been experiencing increase in productivity and improved performance under the leadership of the current chief executive.

Further Data Analysis for Answers to Research Question 4

The research question 4 is restated: Is there any evidence that the increase in productivity and improved performance of the organization has something to do with the integrity of the chief executive? The corresponding hypothesis (Hypothesis 4) states: A chief executive that has integrity will positively influence increase in productivity and improved performance in an organization. The analysis of various data under Neimeth International Pharmaceuticals Plc has revealed lots of evidence and has therefore provided answers to research question 4. In the first place the table 6.4. above shows the chief executive summary scores on integrity measurement as rated by the immediate subordinates using the Perceived Leadership Integrity Scale (PLIS) developed by Craig and Gustafson (1998). The chief executive's average scores fall within the range of 31 to 35 which stands for high ethical. This range is regarded as high level of integrity and therefore proved that the chief executive of Neimeth International Pharmaceuticals PLc has high level of integrity. The interview data analysis, also supports the argument that the chief executive has high level of integrity in so many ways. For example during the interview the chief executive was asked question on his no. 1 strength, and he responded: *"I know that God rewards, so equity and fairness take upper hand – integrity based on the fear of God is No.1."*

He went further to explain and said:

"Integrity has helped me – I receive encouraging letters of commendation from employer and employees telling me that they believe in me and that I did not let them down. It is integrity that drives me. I try to lead by example – if I say that staff should work for 12 hours I must make sure I work for 13 hours."

The above statement is a good confirmation that the chief executive cherishes and values integrity and applies it in his conducts as the chief executive of the organization. He acknowledges that it is integrity that drives him and that he leads by example by ensuring that he works 13 hours when he expects his subordinates to work 12 hours.

From the information gathered from him during the interview and also found in secondary data via the published profile of the organization, he led the management- buy-out of the 60% equity holding of the Pfizer Inc, New York. The buy-out was effected with a loan obtained from Diamond Bank Plc as he reported and it is clear in Nigeria that bank loan for a long-term ventures are usually difficult to secure. The bank trusted him and gave the loan, and he did not disappoint the bank because the loan was fully paid back within a short period. The analysis of the interview data reported above shows a direct link between integrity and the trust by the bank chairman. The chief executive statement in connection with this during the interview is reproduced here:

"Our company subscribes to core values – integrity is cherished, and the fear of God. Our staff are encouraged to try to be the best of what they are, to seek the best for the stakeholders, desire to be fair and seek to protect the interests of the stakeholders. Those who interact with us must see the values."

"This has led Neimeth into privileges and opened doors for the company. The chairman of the bank that gave the loan, said: 'Sam I trust you'. When the last cheque was written the company received commendation from the bank. Bank looks for integrity, and I believe that it opens business opportunity because our company is seen as company of men of integrity – men who keep their words."

In addition to all the facts and evidence already considered for the answer to research question 4, the chief executive of Neimeth International Pharmaceutical Plc, Mazi Sam Ohuabunwa made it clear during the interview that integrity has something to do with the outstanding success of the organization. He was then asked: "Has integrity anything to do with the outstanding success of the organization?" He responded: "It has, because whatever a man sows he reaps". He talked about honesty and went further to elaborate by saying: "In Pfizer, the company subscribes to core values and have entrenched integrity and the fear of God into the system, and expects the staff to demonstrate these values. Before any one is picked up for higher responsibility the management would first look for integrity and industry".

In view of all the above facts and evidence it could be said that the increase in productivity and improved performance of the organization has something to do with the integrity of the chief executive. It is therefore right to say that a chief executive that has integrity will positively influence increase in productivity and improved performance in an organization.

Further data Analysis for Answers to Research question 5

Question 5 restated: Is the suggestion of trait theory that organizations will work better if people in managerial positions have designated leadership profiles valid and applicable in these organizations under investigation?

Hypothesis 5: Organizations in Nigeria will work better and achieve good results if people in leadership positions have integrity.

All the data relating to Neimeth International Pharmaceuticals Plc, such as the interview data on integrity of the chief executive, increase in productivity and growth of the organization, as well as the secondary data have been subjected to some measurement and assessment in order to answer the research questions. The use of PLIS (Craig and Gustafson, 1998) for measurement of integrity, the analyses of the secondary data as well as the interview data proved that the chief executive has high level of integrity and that this has positively influenced the performance in the organization. Besides the answers to research questions 1, 2, 3 and 4 had earlier proved that the chief executive has high level of integrity, and this was confirmed by the immediate subordinates in the organization. The answers to research questions 3 and 4 provided evidence that there were increases in productivity in the organization as practically demonstrated in tables 6.1., 6.2., and 6.3., and that the increases in productivity and improved performance have something to do with the integrity of the chief executive. Integrity could therefore be regarded as one of the designated leadership profiles. It has been proved that it made things happen in this organization because it helped the chief executive of the organization to have positive influence on the staff of the organization, and this in turn made the outstanding performance possible. In view of all the above it could be said that this organization has worked well under the leadership of the current chief executive who proved to possess the leadership profiles.

It could rightly be said that the increase in productivity and the improved performance in Neimeth International Pharmaceuticals Plc could be mainly due to the leadership ability of the chief executive. It is therefore correct to say that a chief executive that has integrity will positively influence increase in productivity and improved performance in an organization. Mr. Sam Ohuabunwa , the chief executive of Neimeth International Pharmaceuticals Plc has reasonably proved both in his leadership qualities and the results he achieved in the organization, that the trait approach to leadership (Northouse, 2001) is applicable in this organization and therefore in Nigeria. The suggestion of trait theory that organizations will work better if people in managerial positions have designated leadership profiles is valid and applicable in Neimeth International Pharmaceuticals Plc. It could therefore be said, judging from the outcome of the investigations in the two establishments, that organizations in Nigeria will work better and achieve good results if people in leadership positions have integrity (Hypothesis 5).

Conclusion

The five research questions have been used independently in reviewing, discussing and evaluating the data presented in this chapter and the results appear very similar to that obtained in chapter 5, concerning NAFDAC. As detailed in chapters five and six above, the questions were effectively answered, and evidences provided were very supportive of the main arguments and were therefore used for conclusions and confirmations in appropriate situations. There were striking similarities in the outcome of the assessment of the data and the answers to the research questions despite the fact that the two organizations were not the same in terms of goals and modus operandi. The NAFDAC is a public-sector organization that is service-oriented (government agency for regulatory services), while Neimeth International Pharmaceuticals Plc is a private sector organization that is profit-oriented and operating in the pharmaceutical industry in Nigeria.

Based on the outcome of the investigations, data presentations, analysis and discussions done in chapters five and six of this work, the main findings are that the two chief executives have high level of integrity and are exemplary leaders with positive influence on their subordinates and outstanding performances in the organizations. The conclusion is that there is a strong relationship between the high- level integrity of the chief executives and the productivity and improved performance of the organizations investigated. It could therefore be said that the integrity of the chief executive could directly influence the leadership outcome like increase in productivity and the growth of the organization. However, there could still be other factors or traits that might have also contributed to the increase in productivity and growth in these organizations. It could also be concluded that integrity is a very important attribute that can help leaders to win the trusts of their subordinates and to lead them effectively to achieve the goals of the organizations. The outcome of these data assessment has helped the researcher to arrive at the final conclusions and the recommendations in chapter seven below. It is important to state that other leaders have a lot to learn from these reports.

CHAPTER SEVEN

CONCLUSIONS AND THE WAY FORWARD

The Nigerian political leaders have consistently failed Nigeria and brought poverty and very slow growth to the nation despite the huge economic potentials and abundant human resources. The major missing link has been proved to be the leadership trait called integrity. The leadership failure in Nigeria and Africa in general has been of great concern and disappointment to all right-thinking and enlightened Nigerians together with all development partners. All are anxious to see Nigeria get out of the self-inflicted doldrum of backwardness, and poor governance, to develop and take her rightful place in the affairs of the world.

There have been so much of wishful thinking and fire-fighting that have been going on without meaningful solution at sight. Concerned Nigerians cannot afford to be complacent on this issue because it is fundamental to any meaningful development in the country. We cannot afford to take "no" for an answer to this great challenge of our time. The challenge may be daunting but not impossible to deal with. It was not known that human beings can be sent to the moon until the Americans gave it a trial. Efforts should therefore continue until we produce effective and exemplary leaders in abundance in Nigeria and Africa.

All hands must be on deck and to whom much is given, much is expected. In line with this thought the author has continued to make his own contribution in leadership development.

He carried out an in-depth research on effective leadership with focus on integrity as a vital trait that could help leaders to achieve desired results in organisations. This proved very relevant and useful for tackling the Nigerian problems. The author looked at the short-comings and weaknesses of the trait theory with the aim of bridging some of the gaps by relating specific trait like integrity to the leadership outcome like productivity or the organisational growth. He used Nigerian organisations to test the validity and the applicability of the suggestion of the trait theory that organisations will work better if people in managerial positions have designated leadership profiles. He carefully selected two successful and well-known Nigerian organisations for the test. The report of the outcome of the test were clearly stated in chapters five and six above. The most exciting of all is the NAFDAC that belongs to public sector where failures are quite rampant. Not only that failures are rampant but NAFDAC itself has not been known for success since inception. This makes it an exciting study. The positive change found in NAFDAC was no magic other than serious impact of the leader's integrity and the ability to win the trust of the followers by the leader. The second organisation selected is from the private sector of the economy and is known as Neimeth International Pharmaceuticals Plc, an off shoot of Pfizer. It also offered opportunity for relevant and an interesting study as reported in chapter six. These reported studies gave strong hope that things could be better if we promote integrity in Nigeria.

1.   The Touch Of God Will Make A Difference

It is very important to remind Nigerians at this point that we cannot eat our cake and have it. A new wine cannot be put into an old bottle without expecting explosion. The leadership expected for the level of change needed in Nigeria can only be possible by divine intervention. Many years of poor political leadership in Nigeria had not only resulted to poor governance and decay of infrastructures, but had promoted corruption at all levels which in turn led to the loss of value system and moral decadence in the society. Our country has low spiritual standards irrespective of the fact that we have more churches and mosques in all our streets. The get-rich-quick syndrome has enveloped the society and '419' business became an industry on its own. Corruption like cancer has destroyed the fabrics of the society. There is corruption at all levels and this affects the way things are done especially in public sector of the economy. Changing and improving political leadership standard in Nigeria is an enormous task that can only be handled by great and rejuvenated minds. No one can give what he or she does not have. Corruption cannot fight corruption. It takes a repentant and renewed mind to do so and it is only God that can change man. We have seen and read about armed robbers changed to great evangelist and leaders by God in our time. Serious repentance is needed in the political space in Nigeria. The Bible makes it clear that without repentance there is no forgiveness. We cannot throw God out of our values and expect to perform wonders. Some great nations have fallen because they said they don't do God. In other words, they feel God is old fashion and unscientific. There is a lesson to learn from these fallen heroes. The fear of God is the beginning of all wisdom. The leadership quality will go up and our country can be great if we acknowledge and respect God in all our dealings in life. The historical facts support this as highlighted in chapter one above. A repentant leader with changed attitude can lead a moral revolution in Nigeria. The unrepentant and recycled corrupt politicians, especially those who emerged through 419 activities lack the ability because they cannot give what they do not have. Nigerians must therefore be thorough in searching for new political leaders that can change the political leadership picture in Nigeria and send waves to other levels of leadership in Nigeria. The emphasis must be on Godliness since this promotes integrity. Godliness with contentment is a great gain (1st Timothy 6:6). This will surely reduce greed and ensure effective utilization of resources for development. Godliness will also help the leader to understand that we brought nothing into this world and certainly will take nothing out (1st Timothy 6:7).

2.   The Research Results On Integrity Should Be Utilized.

The investigations were effectively carried out and the author is excited about the outcome and is happy to announce that there is strong relationship between the high-level integrity of the chief executive and the productivity and the improved performances of the organisations. Integrity was found to be a very important attribute that could help leaders to win the trust of their subordinates for effective performance. The trait theory that organisation will work better if people in managerial position have designated leadership profile was found valid and applicable in Nigerian Organisations. This is therefore sign of hope that we can overcome our leadership problems. More research should be carried out in this field and Nigerian employers and public should begin to make effective use of this research results to improve leadership performance in Nigeria.

3. Integrity Should Be Rewarded All The Time

One thing is very clear about integrity, and that is the fact that it is not common and cheap. Many leaders may have the courage, intelligence and foresight to lead others, but only very few have the required integrity. It is a very scarce attribute that needs a lot of nurturing for it to thrive. It must therefore attract great reward for it to spread in organisations. NAFDAC was not performing well before the appointment of late Professor Dora Akunyili due to corruption but on resumption in 2001 she killed corruption and promoted integrity by rewarding every act of integrity by staff and leading by example. This approach led the subordinates to abandon corruption and compete for integrity because it attracts great rewards. It is likely that corruption has returned to NAFDAC since the exit of Professor Dora Akunyili from the organisation in 2004. It must be stated clearly that Nigeria must be ready to recognise and reward every act of integrity for this to become a new way of doing things in Nigeria. Our nation for some decades now has lost our moral values due to prevalence of corruption in the land as stated earlier. We have witnessed great moral decadence, but integrity has a lot to do with morals. Any one who wants to embrace integrity must drop the filthy gown of immorality. There is need for repentance and God will always forgive and empower the repentant minds. Without repentance it will always be difficult if not impossible. The most effective way to fight corruption in Nigeria and Africa is to promote integrity by attaching rewards to it on continuous basis. Efforts should be made to sustain breakthrough in integrity in organisations by ensuring that succession plans must be made with continuity in mind. It appears that achievement and effective performance at NAFDAC between 2001 and 2004 were not sustained after the departure of Late Professor Dora Akunyili, because fake drugs and expired products have again flooded Nigerian markets.

There is a serious lesson to learn from this if we are to make head way in effective leadership in Nigeria.

4. Integrity Tests At The Entry Points

There should be an integrity test at the entry point for all
those seeking for leadership positions in both public and private sector organisations in Nigeria. This test should be the last
test after the usual aptitude and competence tests because of
the importance attached to integrity. Academic qualification
and ability to pass aptitude test should be regarded as basic
requirements, and success in integrity test should be regarded
as the paramount requirement, because academic excellence
without integrity and character have led to the past failures in
leadership. Simply put, an intelligent leader without integrity,
can easily apply intelligence to smartly exploit and siphon the
wealth of the organisation. Brilliant minds without morals and
integrity will remain an in-house liability.

Having made the points about the importance of integrity in
leadership, we then need to go further by subjecting our leaders
to integrity test. Everybody will easily claim to have integrity
even without any atom of integrity. Verbal claim is no longer
enough, there must be a test to prove and assess the level of
integrity in a leader or anyone aspiring to be a leader. It is
good news, due to research efforts we now have a handy tool
for measuring integrity. We now have Perceived Leader Integrity Scale (PLIS), developed by Craig and Gustafson (1998). It
is indeed a good starting point. The PLIS is based on Utilitar-
ian ethical theory, and attempts to evaluate leader's ethics by
measuring the degree to which subordinates see them as acting
in ways that would produce the greatest good for the greatest
number of people (Northouse 2001). This involves administer-
ing questionnaires and interviewing the immediate subordinates of the leader, and this throws serious searchlight on the
past activities and attitudes of the leader. The questionnaire
contains 31 questions that must be answered by each of the sub-

ordinates and the scores are analysed to determine the level of integrity of the leader. The tool and the calculation process are shown in appendix 1, 2 and 3 below. This tool was effectively applied in establishing the level of integrity of the chief executives of NAFDAC and Neimeth International Pharmaceuticals Plc, as reported in chapters five and six above.

5. The Way Forward For Political Leadership In Nigeria

Political leadership in Nigeria and Africa has remained the major obstacle to leadership development as stated earlier. When the head is rotten the body will surely be dead. The political leadership in a country governs and remains a powerful influence over the entire nation. Unfortunately, the influence has remained negative and corrupt for a long time. The political leaders in Nigeria at local, state and federal government levels have all failed in good governance, but the politicians have been amassing wealth primitively for themselves. This greedy approach to leadership and mindless plundering of the common wealth has brought untold hardship to the citizens.

The poor governance has led to failure of infrastructures and lack of economic growth and development in the land. The citizens have great responsibility to change this poor leadership in the land through democratic means. All hands must be on deck because power belong to the people and it is their right to elect honest people to rule them responsibly. The citizens must wake up from their slumber and be politically educated to take the bull by the horns. The existing corrupt political leaders should be rejected and shown the way out. New aspiring political leaders must be subjected to serious integrity test. Gifts in form of bags of rice, beans, and money during electioneering campaign should henceforth be regarded as taboo and attract rejection and negative judgment by the citizens.

6. Need For Political Awareness And Enlightenment

The citizens should educate themselves and be well prepared to subject the politicians to serious test to ensure that only those who have what it takes to lead will emerge as political leaders in the country. Political leadership is a serious responsibility that requires intelligence, courage, foresight, knowledge, vision and above all, integrity. It is therefore not an area for ordinary job seekers without adequate qualifications. It requires a lot of thinking, planning and strength. The corrupt, weak, sick and very old should not apply because they may not cope well with pressure that is associated with the job. The screening should start with the primary at local government level to ensure that bad materials should not slip through. All the past antecedents of the prospective applicants for political leadership must be examined and queried and answers must be provided by the prospective leaders. Nothing should be hidden or covered up. We must go from the known to the unknown to ensure that people that will receive our votes will not disappoint us again. We need political leaders of great character and not in-competent characters with god fathers behind them waiting to pounce on the wealth of the nation. The journalists and media houses should be very handy and live up to expectation in throwing search lights on the past records of all prospect-ive political leaders. Political propaganda and rhetoric can no longer be sufficient for any politician to scale through. Anyone found to have a dented past should not be allowed to succeed. We strongly need men and women of integrity to lead us out of the wood to the promised land of democratic dividends.

I am delighted and fulfilled to note that my years of research efforts on effective leadership in Nigeria and Africa generally were not in vain. The NAFDAC and NEIMETH studies reported in chapters five and six of this book proved the validity of the trait theory on leadership that organization will work better if people in managerial positions have the designated leadership profiles. I am therefore convinced beyond any doubt based on the above research results that if Nigerian leaders are made to imbibe genuine integrity in their leadership efforts Nigerian fortunes will grow astronomically and poverty will be reduced drastically in the land. We must begin to think outside the box. Nigerians and indeed Africans are encouraged to read this book with an open mind and make their own contributions to ensure that our continent is liberated through effective leadership.

Grants and loans from the developed countries of the world, IMF and World Bank have not done much for Africa for more than fifty years now. Even loans promised by China would not make much difference. These loans and grants had always filtered out and back to their sources because our leaders lack integrity. The donors may not claim ignorance of the situation because they are playing games and their economic interest remains their priority.

Africa and Nigeria need home-made solutions to their problem of underdevelopment. They need internally developed capabilities for total emancipation and transformation. Africa and Nigeria have large numbers of gifted men and women who could turn things around for good. Let integrity be promoted and opportunities given to the men and women who exhibit the virtues of integrity to lead Africa and Nigeria to greatness. Other continents will not give us the development and transformation we are yearning for on a platter of gold. Development and promotion of good leadership quality is the first step for this battle.

THE QUESTIONNAIRES

PERCEIVED LEADER INTEGRITY SCALE (PLIS)

Instructions: Answer all the thirty one questions

Response Choices: 1 Not at all, 2 Some what, 3 Very much, 4 Exactly.

1. Would use my mistakes to attack me personally   1 2 3 4

2. Always gets even   1 2 3 4

3. Gives special favours to certain "pet" employees, but not to me 1 2 3 4

4. Would lie to me   1 2 3 4

5. Would risk me to protect himself/herself in work matters   1 2 3 4

6. Deliberately fuels conflict among employees 1 2 3 4

7. Is evil   1 2 3 4

8. Would use my performance appraisal to criticize me as a person 1 2 3 4

9. Has it in for me   1 2 3 4

10. Would allow me to be blamed for his/her mistakes   1 2 3 4

11. Would falsify records if it would help his/her work situation 1 2 3 4

12. Lacks high morals   1 2 3 4

13. Makes fun of my mistakes instead of coaching me as to how to do my job better   1 2 3 4

14. Would deliberately exaggerate my mistakes to make me

look bad when describing my performance to his/her superiors
1 2 3 4

15. Is vindictive   1 2 3 4

16. Would blame me for his/her own mistake   1 2 3 4

17. Avoids coaching me because he/she wants me to fail 1 2 3
4

18. Would treat me better if I belonged to a different ethnic
group 1 2 3 4

19. Would deliberately distort what I say   1 2 3 4

20. Deliberately makes employees angry at each other 1 2 3 4

21. Is a hypocrite   1 2 3 4

22. Would limit my training opportunities to prevent me from
        advancing 1 2 3 4

23. Would blackmail an employee if he/she thought he/she
        could get away with it   1 2 3 4

24. Enjoys turning down my requests   1 2 3 4

25. Would make trouble for me if I got on his/her bad side 1 2
3 4

26. Would take credit for my ideas   1 2 3 4

27. Would steal from the organization   1 2 3 4

28. Would risk me to get back at someone else   1 2 3 4

29. Would engage in sabotage against the organization 1 2 3 4

30. Would fire people just because he/she doesn't like them if
        she/he could get away with it   1 2 3 4

31. Would do things that violate organizational policy and
then
        expect his/her subordinates to cover for him/her 1 2 3 4

THE MODIFIED QUESTIONNAIRES

THE PERCEIVED LEADER INTEGRITY SCALE (PLIS)

QUESTIONNAIRES - Modified to suit the culture and mode of expression in Nigeria

(FOR ASSESSMENT OF THE LEADER'S INTEGRITY BY THE IMMEDIATE SUBORDINATES)

Instructions: Answer all the thirty one questions

Response Choices: 1 Not at all, 2 Some what, 3 Very much, 4 Exactly.

1. Would use my mistakes to attack me personally   1 2 3 4

2. Retaliates all the time   1 2 3 4

3 Gives special favours to certain "pet" employees, but not to me 1 2 3 4

4. Would like to deceive me   1 2 3 4

5. Would use me as a scapegoat in work matters   1 2 3 4

6. Uses the divide and rule tactics amongst employees 1 2 3 4

7. Is wicked   1 2 3 4

8. Would use my performance appraisal to criticize me as a person 1 2 3 4

9. Is after me   1 2 3 4

10. Would allow me to be blamed for his/her mistakes 1 2 3 4

11. Would falsify records if it would help his/her work situation 1 2 3 4

12. Lacks high morals   1 2 3 4

13. Makes fun of my mistakes instead of coaching me as to how

   to do my job better   1 2 3 4

14. Would deliberately exaggerate my mistakes to make me
look bad when describing my performance to his/her superiors
1 2 3 4

15. Is vindictive   1 2 3 4

16. Would blame me for his/her own mistake   1 2 3 4

17. Avoids coaching me because he/she wants me to fail 1 2 3 4

18. Would treat me better if I belong to a different ethnic group
1 2 3 4

19. Would deliberately misquote me   1 2 3 4

20. Deliberately makes employees angry at each other 1 2 3 4

21. Is a hypocrite   1 2 3 4

22. Would limit my training opportunities to prevent me from
advancing   1 2 3 4

23. Would blackmail an employee if he/she thought he/she
could get away with it   1 2 3 4

24. Enjoys turning down my requests   1 2 3 4

25. Would make trouble for me if I step on his/her toes 1 2 3 4

26. Would take credit for my ideas   1 2 3 4

27. Would steal from the organization   1 2 3 4

28. Would sacrifice me to get back at someone else   1 2 3 4

29. Would engage in sabotage against the organization 1 2 3 4

30. Would fire people just because he/she doesn't like

   them if She/he could get away with it   1 2 3 4

31. Would do things that violate organizational policy and
then

expect his/her subordinates to cover for him/her   1 2 3 4

THE MODIFIED QUESTIONNAIRES

The Perceived Leadership Integrity Scale (PLIS) of Craig and Gustafson (1998) can be used to measure the integrity of the leader or chief executive. This instrument measures subordinates' perceptions of their leaders' integrity in organizational settings. The process requires summing up of all responses on the 31 statements as give above. The lowest and best score is expected to be 31, and indicates that the leader is perceived to be highly ethical, which means high level of integrity. The maximum score on the other hand is expected to be 124, and this will indicate that the leader is perceived to be of low ethical. There are three ranges as follows: 31 – 35   High ethical;

36 – 66   Moderate;

67 – 124   Low ethical.

EXAMPLE FROM NAFDAC DATA ANALYSIS

In answering research question 1, using the above standard and format (PLIS), the questionnaires that were completed by the immediate subordinates to the chief executive at NAFDAC were summarized and analysed as shown below in table 5.2, for the answer to research question 1.

Table 5.2: Summary Scores for PLIS in NAFDAC

Subordinates	1	2	3	4	5	Total	Average
Scores	31	31	33	35	39	169	33.8

APPENDIX 3

(Exhibits 1,2,3,4,5 and 6)

Exhibit 1 – Akunyili (NAFDAC Chief Executive) 2003 Integrity Award

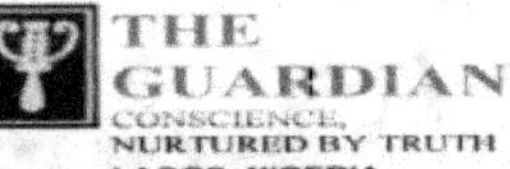

THE
GUARDIAN
CONSCIENCE,
NURTURED BY TRUTH
LAGOS, NIGERIA.
Saturday, May 17 2003

CCM
RECRUITMENT

Click Here!
Opportunities
With Saudi Aramco

Akunyili, Two Others Win 2003 Integrity Award

From Martins Oloja , Abuja

THERE seems to be no end yet to the stream of honours coming the w of the Director-General of National Agency for Food and Drug Administration (NAFDAC), Dr. Dora Nkem Akunyili as she was yesterd named as one of the three winners of the 2003 Integrity Award.

Akunyili who was selected by the global anti-corruption watch dog - Transparency International (TI) will be honoured alongside two other winners. They are former Auditor General of Samoa, Rimoni Ah Chong an Indian, Anna Hazare. Also, a posthumous recognition will be given t Algerian journalist, Abdel Hai Beliardouh and a banker from Mozambiq Antonio Siba-Sibia Macaucua, both of who died fighting corruption.

The cheering news, which was posted on the website of Transparency International TI yesterday, was broken to the Nigerian winner via e-mai from TI office in Berlin Germany.

Akunyili was short-listed on April 27 this year with six others from Bosn Herzegovina, Samoa, South Pacific Region, India, Greece and Poland.

According to the nomination committee. Akunyili was short-listed for the coveted and prestigious award "for her determination to stamp out corr practices in the import and manufacturing of drugs, cosmetics and food products in Nigeria." In recognition of the feat, she has been invited by Transparency International to present a paper titled: Pharmaceutical Security Against Criminal Networks - A Severe Problem In A Poor Cou at the forthcoming International Anti-corruption Conference scheduled · May 25-29, 2003 in Seoul, South Korea.

The Seoul conference will be one of the major highpoints of this year's Integrity Award where Akunyili the other two winners will be honoured.

Akunyili who is the first woman and Nigerian to have won the coveted award was last year honoured at home when she was conferred with o of the Federal Republic of Nigeria (OFR) by President Olusegun Obasa

She has had to her credit about 90 other national and international awa for her relentless drive to eradicate the curse of fake drugs and sanitize regulation and control of drug, food, cosmetics, etc.

"Sua Rimoni Ah Chong, former Auditor General of Samoa, faced death threats when he exposed financial crime at the highest levels of

Exhibit 2 – Receiving of the Anti-corruption Award by NAFDAC Chief Executive

'Head of Nigerian food and drugs agency, Samoan ex-Chief Auditor and campaigner in rural India receive anti-corruption award at International Anti-Corruption Conference in Seoul

Best Investigative Journalism Report on Corruption in Latin America and Caribbean award goes to Nicaraguan journalist

Seoul, 25 May 2003

The Transparency International (TI) Integrity Awards 2003 were awarded today to Dr Dora Akunyili, the Director General of the National Agency for Food and Drugs Administration in Nigeria, Sua Rimoni Ah Chong, the former Controller and Chief Auditor of Samoa, and Anna Hazare, an Indian campaigner against corruption in forestry and in government.

The fourth annual TI Integrity Awards were presented today at the opening ceremony of the 11th International Anti-Corruption Conference (IACC) in Seoul, Korea, hosted by the government of South Korea, on 25-28 May 2003. Transparency International (TI), the world's leading organisation engaged in the fight against corruption, provides the secretariat to the IACC (see http://www.11iacc.org/iacc/index.html). The 11th IACC was opened by Korean President Roh Moo-hyun.

The TI Integrity Awards included special posthumous recognition to Abdelhai Beliardouh, an investigative journalist from Algeria, and Antonio Siba-Siba Macuacua, the chairman of the largest commercial bank in Mozambique, both of whom died while taking a stand against corruption. Valid nominations were received from more than 40 countries.

Dr Dora Akunyili, 48, Director General of Nigeria's National Agency for Food and Drug Administration and Control (NAFDAC) and a pharmacologist by training, has defied death threats while tackling corrupt practices in the manufacturing, import and export of drugs, cosmetics and food products. Since taking up her position in April 2001, Dr Akunyili has earned nationwide respect for her persistence in prosecuting illegal drug traders and in imposing strict standards on multinational companies. In particular, she has pursued manufacturers and importers of counterfeit drugs, deemed to be a leading cause of deaths by stroke and heart failure in Nigeria. Counterfeit drugs worth an estimated US$16 million have been confiscated and destroyed by Dr Akunyili and her staff, in the process saving the lives of thousands of innocent Nigerians. '

Source:http://www.transparency.org/news_room/latest_news/press_releases/2003/2003_05_

25_best_investigative_journalism_award

Exhibit 3–N10 Billion Worth of Fake Drugs Destroyed by NAFDAC in 4 years

NAFDAC DESTROYS N10B FAKE DRUGS IN 4YEARS

Fake drugs and other substandard regulated products worth over N10biliion have been destroyed by NAFDAC in the last four and a half years.

Also over 1,100 container-load of unregistered drugs, processed food and other unwholesome regulated products were impounded by the Agency within the period.

Director-General of NAFDAC, Prof. Dora Akunyili who dropped the hint in a chat with the Abuja Chapter of Nigeria Union of Journalists (NUJ), said that owners of those containers had absconded while a total of 780 raids were carried out by the Agency in various parts of the country between 2002 and 2004.

Prof Akunyili stated that within the period under review, a total of 31 court convictions of accused persons were secured by NAFDAC just as over 40 other cases of violation of NAFDAC laws were pending before the court. Also, about 9,000 sanctions were imposed on offenders within the same period.

She expressed satisfaction that cases of cholera and other water borne diseases have reduced drastically because the Agency had sanitized packaged water production business.

On NAFDAC achievements, the Director-General said: "the entire NAFDAC Laboratories in Oshodi, Kaduna, Maiduguri Yaba, and Port Harcourt are fully automated by our e-lab software. The Agency is in the vanguard of promoting food quality and safety. We have held several workshops. The level of incidence of fake drugs has reduced by over 80% from what it was in 2001. The production capacity of local pharmaceutical industries have increased tremendously while sixteen new drug factories have been established in the last 3 years".

Prof. Akunyili praised President Obasanjo, Honourable Minister of Health, Prof. Eyitayo Lambo and the good people of Nigeria for their overwhelming support for NAFDAC.

She said the Agency will not relent in its efforts to protect public health from the menace of fake drugs and substandard regulated products.

BELGIAN ENVOY LAUDS NAFADAC'S OPERATION

Mr. Dirk Van Eeckhout, the Belgian Ambassador to Nigeria has described the work of National Agency for Food and Drug Administration and Control (NAFDAC) as an important economic intervention and image-making support by the Federal Government.

During his courtesy visit to Prof. Dora Akunyili, Director General of NAFDAC, in Abuja, he described Akunyili as "the right woman for the right job and a true image builder for Nigeria", stating that the European Union has watched with interest how NAFDAC's strict and efficient regulatory activities provided a congenial business environment and strong ties between Nigeria and European nations.

Eeckhout further said that President Olusegun Obasanjo and Akunyili were two of the few patriotic Nigerians who have a good vision for the country.

According to him, the visionary leadership of President Obasanjo and the impressive record of performance by NAFDAC under Akunyili have eroded the wrong conception of European countries that "Nigeria is a country of fraudsters and human traffickers".

Akunyili, in her response expressed the readiness of NAFDAC to facilitate the inflow of foreign investment by Belgian companies as it would create gainful employment for youths.

NAFDAC DG RECEIVES EMRC AWARD

The Belgian European Marketing Research Centre (EMRC) has named the Director-General of National Agency for Food and Drug Administration and Control (NAFDAC), Prof. Dora Akunyili as the Winner of the Agribusiness Award 2005.

Prof. Akunyili is being honoured second time in two years by the Belgian Research Centre for her personal contribution to the promotion of food processing sector both at home and abroad.

President of the Executive Committee of EMRC, Professor Pierre Mathijsen said the Agribusiness Award is in recognition of the "highly professional way and seriousness" with which the NAFDAC Boss has treated the quality of processed food in Nigeria for the past four years.

Professor Mathijsen stated that the award was formally conferred on Prof. Akunyili on April 21, 2005 at the Prestigious Conrad Hotel in Brussels, Belgium where a 3-day international conference on industrialization of agriculture and food processing simultaneously took place.

He commended the Director-General for playing a crucial role in "promoting the potential of Nigeria as a food processing hub and not only as a raw material hangar".

During the award ceremony, Prof. Akunyili presented a technical paper showcasing the country's agricultural and food processing endowment to some potential European investors billed for the Agribusiness international conference.

It would be recalled that two years ago, she was honoured with the Euro Market Award by the same organization.

ANOTHER LAUREL FOR AKUNYILI

Director-General of National Agency for Food and Drug Administration and Control (NAFDAC), Prof. Dora Akunyili has been named the sole recipient of the 2005 Grassroot Human Rights Campaigner Award by the London based Human Rights Defense organization.

The 2005 Grassroot Human Rights Campaigner Award is coming barely one year after Prof. Akunyili was conferred with the 2004 Economic Crime Fighters Award by United Kingdom based ICC Commercial Crime Services Bureau.

Public Relations Director of the International Human Rights Services and Award Ceremony Co-ordinator, Charlotte Morris who broke the cheering news said the NAFDAC Director-General was considered for the 2005 award by some panel of Judges "who admired her direct style and the bravery shown in the face of death threats and assassination attempts in the fight against fake drugs".

Morris observed that Prof. Akunyili's dogged fight against fake drugs has positively changed the fortunes of pharmaceutical industries because until her arrival "importers simply paid a bribe to get their products into Nigerian markets".

He said the award "is a reward for the unsung heroes of human rights who daily risk their lives so that the truth may be heard, the defenceless defended and the powers that be are held to account".

According to him, the award will provide the winners "recognition, protection of a higher profile and a cash sum to further their work and ability to represent their organization".

The official conferment of the coveted award on Prof. Akunyili will take place at the House of Commons Chambers on December 8, 2005 in London and shall be witnessed by some distinguished British parliamentarians, an array of Lawyers, journalists and Human Rights Campaigners across the globe.

It would be recalled that the 2004 edition of the award was won by the Mexican Grassroot Human Rights Campaigner, Esther Chavez and interestingly the NAFDAC Boss is the first African to be so honoured since the award was introduced about 5years ago.

Time magazine award

I agree, Dora Akunyili is a true hero –Obasanjo

JOHN AMEH

PRESIDENT Olusegun Obasanjo has admitted that the influential Time Magazine did not make a mistake in selecting the Director-General of the National Agency for Food and Drug Administration and Control, Prof. Dora Akunyili, as "one of the 18 heroes of our time."

The President spoke in Awka, the Anambra State capital, on Friday, at a luncheon organised for the NAFDAC D-G by the state Governor, Mr Peter Obi, to celebrate her honour.

Obasanjo, who was represented by the Minister for Information and National Orientation, Mr Frank Nweke Jnr, observed that Akunyili was one figure whose contributions to national development had been outstanding in recent years.

The president pointed out that she had implemented the National Drug Policy beyond the expectations of the Federal Government, particularly her relentless war against the marketing of fake and substandard drugs and consumables.

He added that for a woman, who had stuck out her neck in order that others might live, it did not come to him as a surprise that Time Magazine recognised her, moreso at a time she was celebrating her 52nd birthday, adding, "she is indeed, a true hero of our time."

The president assured the D-G that NAFDAC would continue to get all the support it would need to accomplish its goals and responsibilities to Nigerians.

The President of the Senate, Chief Ken Nnamani, described Akunyili as "an example to emulate," but noted that, "it is unfortunate that in our shores, we are more interested in celebrating deviant behaviours."

"One thing President Obasanjo has done well is his ability to identify potential winners in all directions, not minding where they come from.

"I think the nation should begin to think of higher responsibilities for people like Dora in the near future if indeed we want to move ahead", Nnamani added.

Giving his reasons for organising the luncheon, Obi explained that Anambra

Continued on Page 13

'Akunyili is a true hero'

Continued from Page 12

State was turning a new leaf from a state associated with everything bad to celebrate its good indigenes, who had won recognition through hard work and transparency.

He revealed that the state had changed its name from "Home for All" to "Home for All Good People and Light of the Nation."

Responding to the honour done to her by the governor, the NAFDAC boss, who was accompanied to the event by her husband, Dr. Chike Akunyili, and her children, dedicated the Time award to "the NAFDAC Team," which had worked with her since she became the D-G.

"To me, this occasion is not just for eating and drinking but also for thanking God for being picked as one of the 18 heroes of our time.

"Also, that I am alive to be so recognised is by the grace of God. I have stepped on the toes of many merchants of death in the fight against fake drugs and unwholesome products", she spoke in a voice laden with emotion.

Akunyili, an International Star - French Minister

In recognition of her dogged fight against fake drugs and substandard regulated products, the Director-General of National Agency for Food and Drug Administration and Control (NAFDAC), Prof. Dora Akunyili has been described as a "shinning model and international star" worthy of emulation by men and women in public service.

Visiting French Foreign Trade Minister, Mrs. Christine Lagarde who made the remark during her courtesy visit to the NAFDAC Corporate Headquarters in Abuja praised Prof. Akunyili for her valour and courage in daring to wage a vigorous battle against fake Drug Barons even in the face of threats to her life.

Mrs. Lagarde said she was delighted to learn that NAFDAC has created an enabling environment for the importation of more than 88 French pharmaceutical and food products into the country.

The Minister congratulated the NAFDAC Boss for "achieving so much within a short period of time" and pledged the support and co-operation of her home government for the Agency.

She said: "congratulations for doing what you are doing. You are an International star and a shinning model. One of the main purpose of my visit, apart from this courtesy visit, is concerning the multilateral discussions that we will be having in Hong Kong,

because France is very concerned about the access to medicine for developing countries especially those that are suffering from AIDS, Tuberculosis and Malaria".

Mrs. Lagarde further hinted that the French Government was studying all that needed to be done to facilitate greater access to medicine, including the implementation of protocol agreements signed in August 2003 with Developing Countries under World Trade Organization (WTO).

Responding, the Director General of NAFDAC, Prof. Akunyili described the visit of the French Minister "as a rare diplomatic recognition for me, great morale booster, inspiring and motivating gesture" that will spur NAFDAC to greater heights.

Prof. Akunyili disclosed that more than 88 French Drugs and Food products have been registered by the Agency while it currently enjoys a cordial business relationship with over 250 French companies.

She gave a clean bill of health to French pharmaceutical companies as none of them had been found wanting in terms of dealing on fake and counterfeit drugs.

The Director-General appealed to

the French Minister to establish factories in Nigeria because it is a better alternative to importation and source of gainful employment for Nigerians.

Mrs. Lagarde's shower of encomium on the NAFDAC Boss came barely one month after the Portuguese Ambassador, Mrs. Maria de Fatima Perestrello paid her glowing tribute for saving the lives of millions of Nigerians.

BBC Documentary on NAFDAC wins Pulitzer Prize

A British Broadcasting Corporation (BBC) Documentary showcasing the relentless battle being waged against fake drugs in Nigeria by Prof. Dora Akunyili's led National Agency for Food and Drug and Administration and Control (NAFDAC) has won the prestigious Pulitzer Prize for television.

The Award-winning Documentary titled "Bad Medicine" was produced by Veteran Reporter, Olenka Frenkiel and aired on the BBC, widely viewed by millions of its global audience.

Mr. Frenkiel is set to pick up the

coveted prize which is also known as PEABODY AWARD at a colorful ceremony featuring the cream of the world media on 5 June, 2006 in New York, USA.

The star documentary captures how Prof. Dora Akunyili transformed NAFDAC from a near moribund Agency into a formidable fighting force against fake drug Barons and their criminal activities. It also presented the winning strategies adopted by Prof. Akunyili, the attendant challenges and hazards faced by the ebullient Director-General of NAFDAC who has put her life on the firing line in the fight against counterfeit

medicines.

"Bad Medicines", the award-winning BBC documentary is a moving story of how fake drugs endangered the lives of millions of Nigerians and wreaked havoc on the country's healthcare delivery system.

Mr. Frenkiel's choice of NAFDAC's fake drug war under Professor Akunyili has been described as a masterstroke since Akunyili herself had won over 340 national and international awards in recognition of her fight against drug faking and counterfeiting.

References

Achebe, C. (1983), The Trouble with Nigeria, Fourth Dimension Publishers, Enugu.

Adair, J. (1983), Effective Leadership: A Self-Development Manual, Grower Publishing Company Ltd., Grower House Aldershot, Hants, England.

Agbaje, Okunola, and Alarape (2003), Perspective on Positive Leadership in Nigeria: Report of a National Survey, October - December, 2002. Centre For Social Science Research and Development (CSSR&D).

Akanbi M. (2004), "Corruption and the Challenges of governance in Nigeria". Paper presented as the Chairman of ICPC, at the Faculty of Arts Theatre of the University of Lagos, Lagos, on the 19th of August, 2004.

Akunyili, D.N. (2003), Rebuilding Institutions - With Special Emphasis on NAFDAC. A paper presented by Dr Dora N. Akunyili, Director-General, NAFDAC, at The Nigerian Economic Summit, Held at the Nicon Hilton Hotel, Abuja, from 10th September to 12th, 2003.

Akunyili D.N. (2004), "Public Sector Performance - The Case of NAFDAC". A presentation by the Director-General, NAFDAC, at the Lagos Business School Breakfast Club Meeting held on the 6th July, 2004.

Albert I.O. (2003), Mainstreaming, Positive Leadership in Conflict Transformation in Nigeria. Centre For Social Science Research and Development.

Bass, B.M. (1990), Bass and Stogdill's handbook of leadership : A survey of theory and research, New York: Free Press.

Blanchard, Zigarmi and Zigarmi (1985), Leadership and the one minute manager: Increasing Effectiveness Through Situational Leadership. New York: William Morrow.

Bryman, A. (1992), Charisma and Leadership in Organization, London: Sage.

Buchanan D., Body M. and McCalman J. (1988), Getting in, getting on, getting out and getting back, in Bryman A (ed) Doing Research in Organizations. Routledge:London.

CACG (1999), Principles for Corporate governance in the Commonwealth Communication Development Incorporated.

Covey, S. (1992), Principle-Centered Leadership. London, Simon and Schuster, London.

Craig and Gustafson (1998), Perceived Leader Integrity Scale: An instrument for assessing employee perceptions of Leader Integrity. Leadership Quarterly, 9 (2), 127-145.

Cunningham T.M. (2002), Leadership 101: Integrity, US Naval Academy Fire Department, Retrieved 11/9/06, from www.withthecommand.com/2002.Aug/MD-Tmc-leader-integrity 101.html.34k.

Dave Ulrich, Jack Zenger, Norman Smallwood (1999), Result-Based Leadership approach - Leading for attributes and results.

David Richards (1996), Elite Interviewing: Approaches and Pitfalls. Political Studies Association, Published by Blackwell Publishers, Oxford OX4 1JF.

Drucker, Peter F.(1973), Management Tasks, Responsibilities, Practices, New York, Harper & Row.

Eghagha (2003), Reflections on the Portrayal of Leadership in the Contemporary Nigeria Literature. Centre For Social Science Research Development. Positive Leadership Memo graph Series No.6.

Fafowora, O., Tuned AdenIran & Dare O., Nigeria in Search of

Leadership. Spectrum Books Ltd., 1995.

Goleman D. (1998), What Makes a Leader, Harvard Business Review Reprint 98606.

Goleman D., Boyatzis R., McKee A. (2002), Leadership Styles Theory-Vision ary, Coaching, Affiliative, Democratic, Pacesetting and Commanding: Creating Resonance.

Guardian Opinion Poll (2003), Respondents doubt Rulers' Integrity. Retrieved 4/6/2003 from http://news.biafranigeriaworld.com/archive/2003/jun/04/0027.html.

Integrity International (July, 1998).

KirkPatrick and Locke (1991), Leadership: Do Traits Matter? The Executive, 5, 48-60.

Kotter J.P. (1990), A Force for Change: How Leadership Differs from Management. Free Press.

Kouzes and Poster (2002), The Leadership Challenges (3rd Ed.). Jossey-Bass. A Willey Coy, Sam Francisco, Ca.

Lord Devader, and Alliger (1986), A meta-analysis of the relation between personality traits and Leadership perceptions: An application of validity generalisation procedures. Journal of Applied Psychology, 71, 402-410.

Nigerian International Biographical Centre (1999). The New Who is Who in Nigeria. CEDDI Towers, 2nd Floor, 16 Wharf Road, Apapa, Lagos, Nigeria.

ABOUT THE AUTHOR

Isaac Ikem Ngwube. Phd. Fnim

The author's main goal is to develop and empower young and modern leaders to imbibe integrity in their leadership roles and ensure outstanding successes.

"Our research results have proven that integrity is the key attribute for leaders that want to be outstandingly successful".

"He used Nigerian organizations to test the validity and applicability of the suggestion of the trait theory that organizations will work better if people in managerial positions shared designated leadership profiles"

The author, Dr Isaac Ikem Ngwube obtained his PhD from the University of Manchester, UK

www.ingramcontent.com/pod-product-compliance
Lightning Source LLC
Chambersburg PA
CBHW071209240726
48654CB00009B/704